I0459912

For Starters is a book you will want to finish then start to read again. Heather Jo Kennedy presents simple, yet deep, philosophies through easily accessible analogies and relatable anecdotes. For Starters should find a place in every school library and every home.
Bob Kohut - Two Time New Jersey Teacher of the Year

This book had that rare ability to capture my attention and then keep it with a combination of thought-provoking questions, stories and ideas. I feel like the author was having a conversation with me, which was nice.
Martin Hurlburt - The Happy Retirement Guy

Your level of happiness and joy will increase. Your mental health will improve. Your gratitude will grow and your outlook on life will brighten. Heather has a gift, and "For Starters" shines that gift like a beacon in a world that needs more light.
Darrell Holden - Cowboy and Poet

An insightful book and enjoyable read! Heather Jo Kennedy fuses together her IMPACT framework with a variety of stories and anecdotes that are incredibly useful for anyone looking to enhance their performance, improve their game, or simply gain a better outlook on life. Well worth the read!
Brad David Ball - Author

For Starters will give you the insights to see your true identity as a starter and making those fires burn bright!
Shalyse Bellon, High School Basketball Coach

From Youth Starters
I have started to catch a lot of things that I never would have noticed before. This has helped me solidify my identity, feel more grateful, and know who my true team is.
Age 13

This book has helped me a lot to stay true and accountable to my goals and has helped me to set my priorities straight.
Age 19

For Starters
Principles of Productivity You're Overlooking
HJ Kennedy
Copyright © 2025
All rights reserved

This book is protected under the copyright laws of the United States of America. No part of this publication may be reproduced or transmitted in any form or by any means, electronic or mechanical, including photocopying, recording, or by an information storage or retrieval system, without written permission from the author or Cascade Publishing, LLC.

Line/Content Editor: Janelle Evans
Interior Design: Janelle Evans
Formatting: Janelle Evans
Cover Design: Heather Jo Kennedy

1. Self-Help Techniques
2. Education
3. Philosophy

ISBN: 979-8-9901-489-4-9 Trade Paperback
ISBN: 979-8-9901489-3-2 E-Book

Cascade Publishing LLC

Published and Printed in the United States of America

1 2 3 4 5 6 7 8 9 10

Foreword

For Starters guides you through both challenges and opportunities on your journey through self-awareness, personal achievement, and betterment. While keeping a focus on the critical elements of family, relationships, and gratitude in realizing your real potential, Heather takes the hard things that are part of life and applies simple solutions. She illustrates these points through her own life experiences, simultaneously encouraging a shift from what is going *wrong* to what is going *right*.

This book doesn't try to define the next complex strategy in personal leadership and development but instead identifies effective disciplines to use throughout daily interactions with work, family, and friends. The principles in *For Starters* are familiar, easy to understand, and apply.

Col. Michael S. Rapich
Law Enforcement Leader and Administrator

Table of Contents

FOR STARTERS

Principles of Productivity You're Overlooking

So you want to level up? When it comes to increasing productivity and elevating performance, there are valuable skills like organization, goal setting, prioritization, and time management that are common focal points. These are great! But some of the most beneficial principles that promote productivity are a little more subtle. Because of their seeming insignificance, they're often overlooked, but when examined and implemented will have a profound impact on your potential.

Do you have an idea or hope you're struggling to bring to life? Are you feeling like you have more to give but aren't sure what? Are you a team player feeling like you're on the wrong team? Here you'll find resources for discovery, a new perspective on influence, and some undervalued tools that ignite sustainable momentum. And the bonus is…they're easy! In short, this process will make what you do more doable.

Many people have an inner starter bursting to come out, but for various reasons, they get stuck. For Starters is the antidote—a guide to unlocking that stagnation through six powerful focuses. This book is for those seeking to make the difference they were destined to make. It's a reminder of foundational concepts you may have glossed over, but when re-examined and applied, will help you implement steps to maximize your immense potential.

Introduction

Performance and productivity are about more than tools and tricks—they're about igniting a spark that gets you moving and keeps you going. Abraham Lincoln once said, *"If I had six hours to chop down a tree, I'd spend the first four hours sharpening the axe."* Welcome to your axe-sharpening masterclass!

WHAT

For starters... let's work on definitions. What even is a starter?

Many things could come to mind when you hear the word "starter." It's a word that carries big emotion in the sports world. Starters are the first ones to take the field, court, etc. They're the first to play. The general assumption is that they're the best—at least for the team's current objective. In the business world, "starter" could denote entrepreneurship. In a figurative sense, it could refer to someone who's impulsive or gets things done. In a fight, the label of "starter" means the same thing—whether in the street, the ring, or the principal's office, but that's a different kind of book.

✓ Starters use what's available to them to make a lasting change

The common thread in these definitions is the idea of someone pointed in the direction of success and ready to run.

WHO

Originally, I intended this book to be geared toward young adults since many of my clients fall into that category. On the cusp of adulthood, their ambitions and inhibitions are so much fun to coach. But I found myself organically sharing insights from these six principles with colleagues and friends of various ages and realized they have universal application. These points transcend age, gender, orientation, and ethnicity. Anyone, anywhere, at any time can implement any of these concepts and notice a positive change in their levels of performance and productivity. As a bonus, it has proved to me that old dogs *can* learn new tricks!

In close to fifty years of trying to figure out what I want to be when I grow up, I've finally got a lead—I'm a starter. Blessed with countless opportunities to learn and grow in business and personal life, I have crested tops and wallowed in bottoms of many adventures, discovering along the path ways to both make it and break it. From business owner, to coach, to artist, I've covered some ground. I must mention though, it would be remiss for me to not acknowledge almost everything I know I learned from being part of a family.

I loved camping as a kid, and had a father who would take my brothers and I often.

Regardless of where we went, who we were with, or how we slept, there would always be a campfire—the defining quality of a campout. That campfire provided an opportunity for Dad to teach a lesson. He never missed those opportunities.

At a young age he taught me how to build a proper fire. First, we set up the firepit with a hearty amount of dry kindling, then we stacked larger twigs in the traditional teepee formation around the kindling, keeping dry logs to the side at the ready. He coached me on how to allow for some airflow but still have a sturdy structure. I had it down.

One camping trip, he put me to the test in a way I wasn't expecting. As we made our tin-foil dinners, he told me it was my job to set up the campfire. No problem. I quickly went through all the motions I'd learned. As I was wrapping up, he came over holding a single match in his outstretched hand.

"Oh, one more thing," he said, "you get one match. That's it."

No matchbox, no lighter fluid, just a splinter of cheap wood with a tip I prayed was adequate and intact. My mind went immediately back to my preparation. If I'd known I was only getting one match, would I have spent more time constructing the fire? Luckily, he let me revisit my work and you bet I did.

He laid the pressure on thick. "We'll all be real hungry tonight if you don't get it, Heather."

It was an incredible lesson, and oh so good for me on several levels. It illustrated the importance of preparation, patience, and precision. But the reason it was so effective for me personally was... it challenged me.

Now fire-lighting has become a focus of mine.

New projects, like blank canvases, are irresistible to me. I've been blessed with many of those kinds of opportunities to learn and to develop. I've traveled many roads and picked up skills. I've endured a lot of lessons—from piano to sports, to art, to language, even horse-riding lessons (I was a Texas kid, after all). As an adult, I continue to study and take advantage of as much learning as I can. I'm not extra gifted. When people describe me, they may use the word talented because of those skills, but they miss the mark. I'm not more talented or gifted, I'm just productive. And I have an insatiable desire to *start*.

Some of the talents I've developed don't get used as much as they could. But I don't count them as waste, not one bit. If what I've gained from my many ventures can be of any worth to someone else, then it won't be in vain. I've learned some dos and don'ts the hard way and want to share tips so others can be starters of their own fires.

Note that the campfire analogy begins with a search. Depending on where we were camping, there were times the gathering was difficult, where supply was scarce. Such has been my experience with ventures as well. Not everyone has all the resources handy to even begin building let alone light the match. Some tools are better than others and some people are more anxious and ready than others. The process of becoming a starter can be applied across a variety of ambitions, but *ambition* is the key. *For Starters* is intended for individuals who sense they have unmet potential and are ready to get after it.

The trickiest moment in building a fire is the ignition—when your preparation is put to the test. For those of you who think you have what it takes, I've got the match. Let's see.

WHY

There's another word we need to attend to and it happens to be one of my favorites. *Better.* It points to improvement but not perfection, so it's much more productive. Jesus bade of His disciples to, "Be ye therefore perfect." One of the most influential 18th century Bible scholars, Charles Ellicott, translated this phrase as, "Ye therefore shall be perfect," signaling an ideal future state, should we accept all the conditions He laid out. Presuming we can attain perfection while still being mortal is not only naive, it's nonsense. And those who lean toward perfectionism know what a plague it can be. It holds you hostage. Famed academic and researcher, Brené Brown, says that when perfectionism is in the driver's seat, shame rides shotgun. And shame haunts.

On the other end of the perfectionist scale is apathy. From my perspective as a coach, apathetic clients are the most difficult. They give so little to work with. Defiance has an energy that can be manipulated and rerouted. It implies a degree of caring. Apathetic individuals lack care. They're only a step away from hopelessness. But that step is a big one.

In my probing I've found that apathy is often feigned. It's just a cloak that signals avoidance. Dig deep enough and you'll find a care. A spark. Thankfully, I've yet to meet a person without the hint of a spark.

Our goal here is to find the balance between apathy and perfectionism—to make gradual improvements for a better you. That's the attitude of a starter. Starters seek positive change, which is initiated most effectively by desire. You've got to want it. So when given the options of good, better, or best, I say choose better.

Better recognizes a much bigger picture, allowing for setbacks and delays should you mistakenly head the wrong direction. Progress is seldom linear so don't let yourself be thwarted by the tough days. Keep facing forward, even if you're momentarily standing still. Time is constantly passing and taking the sting of failures with it.

Consider the stock market. Full disclosure, I have an arts degree—I know nothing about stocks, but my Certified Financial Planner brother assures me that when my IRA diminishes, it'll recover. Gains and losses are mitigated by time, I just need to chill out and stay the course, because in the end I'll be ahead.

Productive people are like those accounts. Patience is the name of the game. And know this... The better road will be tough. So thicken your skin.

HOW

Quick disclaimer: I am a coach, not a therapist. While there are beneficial suggestions in these pages, if your mental health is questionable, seek a licensed, medical professional for help first.

In my coaching I've found a specific pattern to be both effective and maintainable. It consists of three actions:

1. Find one thing to eliminate.
2. Find one thing to embrace.
3. Find one thing to consider.

Think traffic lights. Red lights signal to stop, to apply the brakes. Green is your indicator to leave that red light behind and get moving, nothing in your way. Yellow is a judgment call. Attitudes toward yellow vary greatly depending on personalities. For the purposes of these productivity points, yellow will indicate something you need to consider or apply more questioning to. Many great discoveries and movements started with a question. Each of these steps needs your personal judgment.

If you choose to use this as a workbook, there is a workspace at the end of each chapter. Take advantage of that space to write notes. Do the work.

A psychology professor at Dominican University in California performed a study with 267 participants and concluded that simply writing goals down increases your chances of success by 42%[1]. Take that edge! If it's not measurable it's not movement, so use these actions as your measuring tool for productivity. Make three daily goals—something to stop, something to accelerate on, and something to question.

Directionally, these principles are more arbitrary than incremental. If one feels sticky, jump to another and come back later. I like a kind of flexibility that appeals to whichever brain hemisphere you favor. Call me inclusive.

To make the most of the suggestions in this book, take one week for each step. Focus on that step. Get in the habit of recognizing where you can improve and where you're succeeding. Refine the step until you feel like it comes naturally. Spoiler, these steps are all natural. They may be uncomfortable, but they're basic, organic, and implementable. If you find yourself uneasy about one of them, that's a good sign. It means you have something to attack—a project! Projects lead to progress. But you can trust that these steps are wholly beneficial (in moderation... as with anything).

They are simple, so much that they get overlooked, and that's the rub. If you attend to them prayerfully and with full intent, you will become a more productive, more peaceful, more fulfilled, and a more accomplished person. You'll be better.

Now let's get started.

Gratitude Frees You and Feeds You

"So remember Me; I will remember you."
QuRan, Surah Al-Baqarah (2:152)

How does a starter begin the day? With gratitude. It is the first and most essential tool for starting strong. It establishes a mindset for fueling progress.Granted some of us are innately "morning people". This isn't so much how you *feel* about the morning, it's what you *do* about the morning. Starters don't avoid the morning, they attack the morning. So regardless of what time you start your day, start strong. If you're a morning-struggler, this step is a great way to attack it without overburdening yourself.

✓ Starters are grateful

You may not have a single follower on social media or a dollar in your bank account. But if you think you're starting from scratch, you are dead wrong. You have history, knowledge, experience. You have a whole world under your feet. You have feet! If you don't, you certainly have a brain that can comprehend inspirational self-help books. And if you're reading this particular book, whether you've identified it or not, you probably have a reason. But don't sweat about that yet.

Forget about your projects for a bit. Put them on the shelf and don't worry about your why at present. First thing's first, you must develop the characteristics that will allow you to achieve those goals.

We begin with gratitude. At the very least, when you wake up and before you get into bed, you *must* count your blessings. There is power in thankfulness that you can find nowhere else. Trust me on this. It's step one on purpose.

BENEFITS

Starters are clear on what they desire because they're clear on what they've been given. Gratitude propels them in ways nothing else can. Regular practice of gratitude has been linked to immense benefits, including mental, social, and physical advantages.

Mental
- Grateful people experience significantly better mental health.[2]
- Gratitude helps to reduce toxic emotions, from envy and resentment to frustration and regret. It can even shift one's mental focus away from negativity, contributing to greater life satisfaction and optimism.[3]
- Gratitude improves self esteem. It increases resilience and emotional intelligence, and happiness.[4]
- Gratitude has been shown to alleviate anxiety, grief, and depression.[5]
- Other studies reveal improved resilience[6] and patience.

Social
- Saying "thank you" leads to new social opportunities.[7]
- Gratitude is linked to lower levels of aggression.[8]
- Gratitude can yield lasting changes in brain function, helping individuals become more inclined toward generosity and positive social interactions.[9]
- Other research has indicated increased forgiveness, vitality, better relationships and less jealousy. If you

and your partner show regular appreciation for each other, you're more likely to stay together long-term.[10]

Physical
- Grateful people are physically healthier. Gratitude can contribute to lower blood pressure, glycemic control, asthma control and even eating behaviors.[11]
- Gratitude improves immune function and reduces inflammation and anxiety.[12]
- Gratitude significantly lowers feelings of stress and fatigue.[13]
- Grateful individuals experience improved quality of sleep.[14]

Spiritual
- Grateful people have a heightened sense of belonging and well-being.[15]
- Gratitude fosters humility.[16]
- There is a positive link between gratitude and spirituality/religiosity.[17]
- Gratitude improves an individual's sense of meaning.[18]
- Gratitude encourages focus on the present moment, leading to increased mindfulness.[19]

THREE GOOD THINGS:

"Three Good Things" is a practice I learned from my doctor. After our third baby, I had minor postpartum blues so he recommended this behavioral remedy he'd learned about from Duke University.[20] It's a positive psychology technique that rewires the brain.

Here's an abbreviated version of what it involves: Each night before you go to bed you reflect on the events of the day and write down three positive things that happened that day. Our brains

11

are biologically coded to reflect on the negative aspects of the day—it's what helps us survive as a species—but, unfortunately, this tendency to highlight the negative can lead to depression and burnout.

After only one week of participating in the study, individuals reported increased happiness and a better ability to identify positive things in their lives. After two weeks of consistent effort, people were generally happier and more peaceful than those who didn't and for a longer duration than people who took prescription anti-depressants.[21]

Personally, I experienced similar results, so much so that I've implemented it now in our family. With anxiety, stress and depression on the rise in young people, I am bringing every precaution I can. So every night when I tuck my kids into bed, (if I'm too tired, I'll admit—they tuck me in) I ask them to tell me their three good things. In the Kennedy vernacular, though, we call them our "three cookies."

COUNTING COOKIES

At our house, there is a deep and abiding appreciation for warm, home-baked cookies. In an attempt to satisfy-yet-ration our obsession, we have established a "cookie day" once a week. It began when they were in grade school and each Wednesday was a short school day. We decided making cookies would make it extra fun. And it was even more special because they got to enjoy my parental attempt at abating obsessive portion-control tendencies. My role (besides baker) was to let them indulge freely! Well...I tried.

At one point on a particular day, however, my "mom-stincts" emerged. In a moment of weakness (or strength—you decide) I cut them off after they had three cookies each. The ensuing devastation was momentous. The poor, poor, deprived children gave an impressive performance of their pitiful living circumstances.

12

I mean, how dare I deprive them of their one and only piece of happiness in their sad little lives? So, with the creation of "Cookie Day" we inadvertently gave birth to "Fourth Cookie Syndrome."

Fourth cookie syndrome: the depressed state of an individual denied an additional blessing... after prior indulgence in several.

Do we do this sometimes? Do we complain about circumstances when we should be feeling gratitude?

At any given moment, there is something to be grateful for, so especially in times of frustration, a conscious recognition of such is beneficial.

The first time I remember recognizing this concept, I was a teenager. I'd sprained my ankle in a volleyball game, and the pain was intense. Kneeling to say my prayers before bed, I could hardly tolerate the throbbing. I tried forcing myself to focus on the parts of my body that were not in pain. It didn't ease the pain in my ankle but it did reroute my focus, which helped me cope. Then and there I promised God that when my ankle was healed, I would go out of my way to realize when it *wasn't* hurting. And I do! Over thirty years later I say random prayers of gratitude for an ankle that is pain-free.

Gratitude has a silent strength that is too often untapped.

Next time you find yourself upset about something, take a deep breath. Look around at all the cookies you've had. Count them. Don't let the denial of one thing ruin the enjoyment you received from previous blessings.

COMPLAINTS

In theory, the three-good-things practice is simple and effective. But those who live in families know the "theory" is never the status quo. In my *real-world* experience from implementing cookie-counting with my kids at bedtime, I notice that sometimes they

13

can't think of anything to be grateful for. Some days just stink. (Sometimes, it's just the hour or two before bedtime that really stinks and that clouds remembrance.)

This is when I ask them to complain. Stay with me—it's a trick. I am a parent after all.

Think of the last time you complained. For you goody-goodies who don't complain, when did you feel annoyed or frustrated? If you don't get annoyed…I've got nothing. Move to the next chapter, you're all good here. Otherwise, what was your last complaint about? Go to that moment in your mind. Where were you? Who was with you? What were the circumstances? Fill in the blank:

I was upset because _____.

Now, step outside those feelings and look for some aspect of this particular situation that's a blessing. Somewhere in that underlined segment is a privilege. Here's where we make the switch. Though there are many times when we struggle to vocalize our gratitude it's almost always easy to find something to complain about. And behind every complaint, you'll find an entitlement. I've yet to find an exception.

This won't solve whatever problem you're facing at the moment, but the mindset shift is liberating not only for you, but those around you as well. So when you can't think of anything to be grateful for, think of a complaint instead. Peel away that complaint to find the privilege. Once you make the realization, shift to gratitude. Here are some examples:

"There's nothing to eat."
Do you have abilities and resources? Have you eaten in the last twelve hours? Will there be an opportunity within the next twelve hours for you to eat? Maybe there's not a convenient, immediate palate-pleasing option for your taste, but if you aren't suffering from legitimate starvation, be thankful for that.

14

"I'm stuck in traffic."

Are you in a vehicle? Is it working? Playing music? Is there temperature control? You may be late for an appointment or inconvenienced in your atmosphere, but there are so many entitlements in this phrase.

"I can't make the party. I have to work instead."

Do you have a job? Does someone trust you enough to pay you to do work? Employment is not only a privilege, it's also an opportunity for growth in many ways, no matter the occupation. Parties are overrated anyway.

"My bed is uncomfortable."

Our family met the sweetest, happiest girl in Mexico a couple years ago who showed us her "room." It was actually just a corner of the one-room shack. Her bed was a piece of plywood, not quite a meter in length.

Now you try...

There are too many ads on this streaming service.
I don't have time for this.
I'm broke.
This porridge is too cold.

These may seem smug or dismissive, that's not my intention. But beware of the *"I'll be happy when"* mentality. It's a trap. Proactively choose happiness with gratitude. Life hands us lemons and sometimes we just need to wallow in that sourness. However, we must make sure our wallowing is temporary. Because here is a hard truth. At some point everyone who walks this earth will get kicked down. Too many people face challenges far greater than a traffic jam or an empty fridge. Recognizing this can help us shift complaints into gratitude for what we do have.

- In 2022, reports showed over 580,000 people in the

United States experienced homelessness.[22]
- In 2022, 44.2 million people in the US alone didn't have enough food. 13 million of those were children.[23]

You will experience nightmares, loss, and heartache. But you'll also experience daydreams, gain, and peace. Complainers and critics remain unhappy while starters are able to move on.

- In 2023, reports indicated that over 36,000 permanent housing units, including supportive housing and rapid rehousing options, were added to the national inventory.[24]
- In 2022, 49 million people received charitable food assistance. Food pantries have been estimated to annually contribute $28 billion nationwide.[25]

I have always loved this quote from Jenkin Lloyd Jones:
"Anyone who imagines that bliss is normal is going to waste a lot of time running around shouting that he's been robbed. The fact is that most putts don't drop. Most beef is tough. Most children grow up to be just ordinary people. Most successful marriages require a high degree of mutual toleration. Most jobs are more often dull than otherwise. Life is like an old-time rail journey—delays, sidetracks, smoke, dust, cinders, and jolts, interspersed only occasionally by beautiful vistas and thrilling bursts of speed. The trick is to thank the Lord for letting you have the ride."

It's difficult to break the habit of complaining, but like any other habit the first step is recognition. The next step is taking control, finding a solution or at minimum…a cookie. If you want another trick, try this. Set a stopwatch on your phone and see how long you can go without complaining. When you catch yourself in a complaint, restart the stopwatch. In a 24-hour period, how long can you go between complaints? Set a goal to improve that time each day.

There will be times when your porridge will be too cold. The point where you make the shift to gratitude is critical. Use these tricks to give yourself an advantage. Let your complaints lead you to what you've been enjoying yet remiss in recognizing. Let them lead you to the more productive response of identifying solutions instead of problems.

SUMMARY

In the New Testament, Christians read about an encounter between ten lepers and Jesus Christ. Though the ten were all healed, only one was "made whole." (King James Version Bible. 1993. Luke 17:19) You may want healing. You may need healing. And you may get it. But how do we attain wholeness? The difference was and still is gratitude.

Austrian psychologist, neurologist, and survivor of three Holocaust concentration camps, Viktor Frankl, taught us that "Everything can be taken from a man, but one thing: the last of the human freeoms–to choose one's attitude."

Do not let step one be an obstacle. It's too easy to accomplish. Develop a grateful heart by letting go of complaints and recognizing all the beautiful cookies in your life. Let vitamin G be your most important daily vitamin because few things will help you more than beginning and ending each day giving thanks, and spreading as much thankfulness throughout the day as you can.

From here on, each succeeding principle will include warnings. But there is really no way you can mess up when it comes to realizing or giving thanks. I try to be careful with words like "always" and "never" but there is truly always something for starters to be grateful for. Always.

Identity Is the Bedrock of Your Impact

"I am not who you think I am; I am not who I think I am; I am who I think you think I am."
Charles Cooley

Lesson one in identity—you are not who others say you are. This quote from an American sociologist underscores a harsh reality. Too often people tend to let others define them. Others may have some influence, but who you are at your core is none of their business.

NATURE AND NURTURE

Our family was on a long road trip through the Great Basin Desert. My husband, Kelly, was at the wheel. I sat sleepily next to him with our four kids in the back. During one particularly remote section of the trip, nothing but sand and rocks in sight, something stirred me from my daze. Up ahead, on the side of the road, I noticed movement. Coming back into coherence, I sat up to hone in on what I was seeing. I realized Kelly had noticed it too when he started slowing the car down. As we got closer, we could tell it was small, and seemed to be some sort of live animal, but we couldn't be sure. Kelly flipped on the hazard lights and pulled off the road. As I opened my door, I saw the tiniest baby puppy with matted tan fur and the sweetest smoky black muzzle. It couldn't have been more than two weeks old.

We didn't have a plan, but we do have hearts. We couldn't just drive on. Softly approaching this pitiful animal, I did my best to not wonder what circumstances could have brought it here. Instead, I began picturing images of rehabilitated animals turned cherished

23

pets. In fact, I knew of a reputable animal sanctuary only a couple towns away from where we were. It was time to save this thing and go home heroes. However, such images were not going through the puppy's mind. It bared its teeth and growled, backing away steadily at our approach. Clearly, this was not going to be a grab-and-go situation.

Bait, that's what we needed. We had startled the poor thing. So I walked back to the car and grabbed a Slim Jim, because what creature lost in the desert would be able to resist a Slim Jim? I peeled the plastic back to expose the beefy aroma. Crouching down I inched toward the puppy again. It held its combative stance and wasn't looking to change its mind. Just then, I saw out of the corner of my eye more movement near some sagebrush. I couldn't believe what I saw. There was another puppy.

We fared no better with the second one. It had to have been from the same litter. Not only did it share the same coloring and size, but the same nasty attitude as well. It wouldn't let us anywhere near. Only a few seconds passed before they teamed up and ran under a sagebrush. Even under the protection of the bush, they didn't stop growling at us. Now we had to make a decision. There was no way these babies were going to survive out here. But with four children in the back of our car and no foreseeable way to tame the ferocity out of the puppies, we couldn't responsibly complete the rescue I'd imagined. So in real disappointment, we headed back to the car and went on our way.

I'm not sure why it took so long. Maybe it was the delusional desert void, but several hours and many miles later it occurred to my husband and I that those were not in fact puppies. They were coyotes. Though we were slow to the game, they knew all along exactly who, what, and where they were. Even in their infancy. They weren't lost in the desert—they owned the desert. And no strange lady with a Slim Jim was going to convince them otherwise.

Each human is born from a unique equation that includes both biological and environmental components. We are a product of our DNA and our culture, or in more familiar terms, nature and nurture.

More to come on nurture, but to tap into your nature, do not mistakenly consult the community. They're part of your nurture, your environment, your village. Nature really has nothing to do with them. It's time to do some soul-searching and self-reflection. Learn about you, write down things you notice about yourself, your likes and dislikes. Knowing who you are is critically linked to your productivity.

———— • ————

Do you enjoy people-watching? It's remarkable how individually different we can be as a species. So, I was alarmed to discover that 99.9% of genetic arrangement (DNA) is the same for all humans. "Between any two humans, the amount of genetic variation—biochemical individuality—is about 0.1 percent. This means that about one base pair [of DNA] out of every 1,000 will be different between any two individuals."[26] In non-science terms, the building blocks of humans are all so similar that under a microscope the difference between any two humans is almost indiscernible. Can you believe that? *Any* two humans. We have so much more in common than apart.

I love this reminder that as a species our similarities grossly outweigh our differences. I hope for the day when we treat one another as the brothers and sisters we are, but we really do like to hone in on those differences. Because what a vast 0.1 percent, right? And those differences matter.

You are unique, individual, and original. You and all those around you have strengths and weaknesses, likes and dislikes, and a whole slew of special traits which have nothing to do with how, where, and with whom you were raised. This is the "nature" part of the identity equation. The other part of your equation, the "nurture" part, deals with how your circle of influence affects your individuality. This is why your team matters deeply. We'll get there.

First, I want you to think about someone you love so much it hurts. See if you can quantify how much you love them. How far could you run for them? How much money would you give for them? How long would you wait for them? Really try to assign numbers in answer to these questions. Really explore how deep that love goes.

Now ask yourself this: How far could you run, how much would you give, how long would you wait... for you? Let's don't forget that the principal member of a personal team is self. Sure, you've probably heard about the non-existent "i" in "team", but if *I* am not a part of it, it's not *my* team. We have to understand who we are to the core, in order to build the right relationships around us. Personal identity is the foundation for your team. So learn to listen to your own voice. Is it critical or supportive? Do you have grace for yourself like you would a friend? How you feel about you is where identity starts.

———— • ————

I spent my childhood just north of Dallas, Texas. Not exactly the "deep south" but that strong Texas twang was ubiquitous, and I was a ripe candidate for picking it up. I love watching old home videos of my brothers and I as kids and hearing the slow, melodic southern drawl that naturally developed from living there. But at fourteen years old I moved with my family to Arizona. My new friends and acquaintances were quick to notice the funny way I spoke. Their comments identified me as an outsider and all my teenage self wanted was to blend in. It didn't take me long to shed those down-home Texas phrases and adopt a more "normal" lingo. To this day it's one of my biggest regrets.

Many years later, living in Utah, I had a neighbor from the South who had a strong southern accent. It took me back to my roots, and when I talked to her I sometimes felt my own voice slipping back into the twang of my youth. I was startled as I got to know her that she'd been away from the South for over twenty years. Unlike mine, her accent had stuck.

Why did I conform to my environment and why didn't she? Did she have a stronger personality? Was my nature weak? It's not that simple. I had a fear of labels and being known as "Southern" or "the girl that talks funny" was not going to help me blend in so I forced a change.

Both intrinsic and influenced aspects of identity can be adjusted. Change can be positive, negative, or it can be simply change. Positive changes are worthy of celebration. The indicators will be growth and strength. But when change is negative, the result or indicator will be loss of identity. The trigger for this negative change is usually the same. **Comparison** is the most likely culprit.

Comparison is a subtle yet deceptive gauge of status. It's a tool alright—a vice with a grip that drags you to self-vacancy. Comparison only shows up when identity is in question. If you're sure of who you are, you have no reason to judge your identity against others. When you find yourself comparing, train yourself to stop. Stop scrolling on social media and go read your journal. Stop staring out the window and go back to the mirror. You'll never find yourself when you're looking at others. Identity is realized in the quiet times you spend alone. Check with God, check yourself. It's not change that we need to avoid, but the pull to compare.

Data from UNESCO shows that around 600 languages have disappeared in the last century. If that trend continues, by the end of the century we could lose up to 90% of the world's languages.[27] Though I'm partly to blame for not perpetuating it, I still have hope we don't lose *Texan*.

PERFECT
Besides comparison, another practice that needs to be avoided

for the sake of identity is **perfectionism.**

One Sunday morning, on our way to church, my then nine-year-old calmly asked from the back seat if she could borrow my phone for "something." We were all dressed, fed, loaded, buckled, and slated to be on time, so feeling obliviously content about our smooth morning, I passed the phone back to her, unsuspecting of any hiccups this late in the game.

But after a few minutes the phone came back to me with a picture on it. It was of her tights...with a giant hole in the knee. Scribbled on the image was a mark-up with the word "oops" and a squiggly smiley face. Knowing the tights were intact when she entered the car only minutes before, I asked her what happened. After some initial hesitation she gave all the explanation our car full of girls needed, "Um," she said, "there was a string."

Immediately understanding, I offered no solution or lecture, just an affirming, "Dang, sis."

Loose strings capture us too often as we fixate on their defiance. By the time we realize we've been tugging and pulling at the problem instead of the solution, the damage is done. In figurative terms, this issue begs the question, What are your strings? What flaws are you chasing? *Recognizing* weakness is a vital step in progression and productivity. *Fixation* on weakness is not.

Growing up in a celebrity family had its curses. I was trained from a young age to focus on how I was perceived. Ever image-conscious, I paid too much attention to how others might view me or my actions and went to extreme lengths to exude the perfect child, student, athlete, attendee, etc. Worrying about what others thought became an obsession to the point where I felt my very safety and the safety of my family was in jeopardy if I misbehaved. While you may not have this degree of anxiety regarding perception, I would wager you think about how others view you more than you realize. How much time do you prepare getting ready for the day versus ready for bed? Where are your thoughts pointed when doing either?

While this error of my youth had a small degree of benefit, in large part it became a plague. It's taken years for me to understand that part of being self-sufficient is to free yourself from the bondage of others' judgements. Most often we're wrong about what others are thinking anyway.

My daughter taught me a phrase I've adopted when a decision is made. She was in her bedroom trying to pick an outfit for a party. I wasn't immediately available and held her off until I had the time to give my full attention. By the time I got to her, she'd made her selection. When I tried to offer my approval, she held up a prohibiting outstretched hand, "All opinions are no longer valued." I probably should have been offended, but I wasn't. I was amazed and inspired. She had decided, and no influence was going to surpass the approval she gave herself.

Worrying about what others think is one way we let perfectionism incapacitate us, another way is indecision. What causes the paralysis of choice is the anticipation of only two outcomes: success or failure. But what if those weren't the only two possibilities?

What if we consider each step an opportunity rather than right or wrong? Sure, some choices will generate better results than others, but every choice is not so black and white. Even with a wrong step, the opportunity for success is not lost... if by *success* you mean *progress*. (That's a word-switch you may need to make.)

This can be frustrating counsel. We want to know exactly what needs to be done so we can do it perfectly. Ambiguity to a perfectionist is headlights to a deer and a bane to someone who can't seem to pull the trigger. But when faced with choices, not choosing can be an equally detrimental choice.

Perfectionism exists because of expectations. We must learn to be careful with expectations and the narrow-minded idea that only two outcomes exist. Just take a step. When you're in search of progress, you'll recognize when something is off. There will be indicators. Trust that, and trust that those *wrong* roads, while costly, can yield profound benefits and value—often as much as the *right* roads. Without some mis-steps it's difficult to confirm the *right* ones. So if you make some bad turns, relax and reroute. Don't ever adopt the "it's too late" language. Starters don't get stuck for long.

———— • ————

Masked snug behind perfectionism is often an insidious little creature called **doubt**. While questions and doubt can be productive, self-doubt never is. As a chronic questioner, I've learned this surprising insight about doubt; even evidence and experience cannot dispel it.

How is that possible, though? If doubt is essentially 'uncertainty or lack of conviction' then obtaining certainty or conviction should eradicate it, right?

It doesn't work that way. Why? Because doubt is irrational. It doesn't follow rules, because it doesn't actually exist. It is only present in the feeble mind wherein it resides. Doubt doesn't exist until you give it credence. This is the clue that leads us to the antidote.

The way to remove doubt is first, to challenge it. Self-doubt is no exception. Turn the tables and stare it down. Ask where it's coming from or what ground it stands on. Defend yourself from your most dangerous critic—you. Having an honest perception of yourself includes recognizing your limits and weaknesses so when those imperfections appear in the mirror you can take them standing up.

Then, consider perfectionism again. The nagging criticism born from perfection feeds the doubt that validates the criticism. It's an endless and damning cycle. Looking outside yourself can eliminate its oppression even if temporarily. Find a way to focus on serving others instead of adhering to the nit-picky voices begging you to look inward.

Comparison and perfectionism may offer a momentary boost to progress, but you can depend on both to significantly stifle your identity.

Eradicate them.

REASON

I've already mentioned the importance of having a **reason**. Your reason fuels your goal. Simon Sinek calls it your *why*. In the fire-building analogy, it is possible to set up a perfectly designed campfire. With just the right amount of kindling structured among larger, dry logs, you can get a single match to take. But any wind, collapse, or other anomaly and your fire is out. At the first sign of strain, it dies. With an abundant source of fuel, you have sustenance. Your *why* is your personal fuel.

We'll do a deeper dive on reasons in the section on action. For those of you who have identified yours, congratulations. For those of you who haven't, how do you find it? You're beginning to tap into it with gratitude. You'll start to notice common themes in your thankfulness practice. What you appreciate points to your values. Values fuel your reasons. Notice what your grateful items have in common. Notice the common themes.

Here's an example. Let's say you've been counting cookies and writing down every day what you're grateful for.

"Dinner was good tonight."

"I found a cute new breakfast spot."

"Mangoes were ripe."

It would appear you value food, right? Yes, but digging a little deeper we continue to find core values. Being grateful for food could come from valuing creation, art, experiences. Looking at the rest of the list you see.

"It's time for bed."

"I took a warm bath."

"I got new sweatpants."

An underlying value in this case could also be comfort. Good

31

food holds value because it provides comfort. If you're digging for gold and you find a clue, for goodness sake keep digging. Once you identify the *why*, it will start to become more obvious. You'll begin to notice all the other aspects of your life that support your core values. These reasons and values are a base part of your identity.

To dial in on your reasons, begin with gratitude. Then take a good look at your strengths and weaknesses. There are plenty of assessments online–find one and see how you feel about the accuracy. You don't have to fully buy into the results. Question them. A lot of personality assessments don't earn much credence from me, but that doesn't mean there's not potential for discovery. Find a balance between skepticism and openness to reveal truths about who you are to the core.

Mom always said, "There's no one else in the world just like you." That never impressed me much until I thought about the 0.1%. With eight billion brothers and sisters filling a 0.1% spread, that's a small space in this world to occupy. And yet no other person has the unique traits, tendencies, and abilities you do. And no one has the same desires. It's at once impossible to comprehend, but impossible to deny. We are all here for a cause, and each of us has one thing in common with everyone on earth—unmatched potential.

Values fuel reason, and reason drives success.

Loved ones often provide the best reasons. As previously determined, we do things we never imagined when love gets involved. Remember to measure the distance you would go for a loved one, then apply that distance to yourself.

HOBBIES

✓ Starters are creators

Here's some irony. I didn't find myself until I stopped looking so hard. Of all the relationships you'll have, the most important and influential one will be with your Maker. Whatever your beliefs, acknowledge something higher and purer than yourself and be sure you are at peace with that entity. Remember, your identity is no one else's business but yours and your creator's.

The idea of starting has spiritual roots. In fact, faith is the foundation of starting. If we didn't believe something could come of nothing, why would we bother starting anything at all? The creation of the world not only gave us life but gave us a model for becoming creators ourselves. Our diverse abilities to create and innovate separate us from the other species, yet most of us don't embrace that ability as we should. There have been a handful of times when I've felt *called* to create something. I've yoked myself to heaven and sought continued divine guidance throughout the process. Those projects have been far and away the most rewarding. Allowing yourself to be a tool in the hands of a greater source is transcendent. It shapes you permanently.

HOBBIES HELP YOU **DO**. CREATIVE HOBBIES HELP YOU **BECOME**.

Everyone in this world has not just one but multiple gifts to give. Our relationships are vital to our identity. Often those closest to us see our gifts before we are aware of them. Some gifts may be inherent and obvious, others more hidden. Either way, they need to be identified and cultivated.

Though the topic here is productivity, you must understand that producing is not the same as creating. Interview second graders and you'll find aspiring creators. They crave creation. At some point in their worldly education and progression, however, they lose that drive. Those dreams get pushed aside to make room for "more important" aspirations. But it's those intrinsic creative tendencies that help us find our gifts. And what could be more important than that?

- A 2012 study examined the health and longevity of over 1,000 older adults and found that those engaged in creative pursuits experienced a 13% reduction in mortality risk.[28]
- A study in 2016 found that "positive association with gardening was observed for a wide range of health outcomes, such as reductions in depression and anxiety symptoms, stress, mood disturbance, and BMI, as well as increases in quality of life, sense of community, physical activity levels, and cognitive function."[29]

Creative work often involves solving novel problems, continuous learning, and social engagement, all of which have been shown to support brain health and reduce the risk of dementia. Artists, musicians, and inventors often keep mentally and socially active, which can be beneficial for longevity.

What are your **creative hobbies**? Are you making time to develop them? If you don't have any, find something that interests you. Try a lot of things and see what feels right. Maybe you aren't musical or artistic, that's not a problem. Learn coding, practice photography, design a new play for your basketball team or try new ingredients in your milkshake. There are countless opportunities to create. Hobbies help strengthen your identity and fill a spiritual hunger. Participating in any creative act is a sacred experience and should be treated with reverence. If you still lean toward perfection, the Greek word for *perfect* means finished or complete. In other words, fully developed. I like to term it as "gifts maximized".

I have spent countless hours invested in art and music. With both, I was able to achieve a professional level and make them into side-businesses. I taught music for twenty years and loved it. When family obligations grew, I stepped away to focus on our kids and help Kelly with our other business. The same happened with my art. I was able to collaborate in some incredible projects, participate in shows and sell some commissions. But one tired evening as a commission deadline approached, I found myself complaining to Kelly about the time I would have to spend to get it done on time. Knowing how overwhelmed I was, he gently suggested I stop trying to make painting a business and keep it as a hobby. I love painting, but monetizing it was killing the passion. As soon as he said the words, I felt a weight lift from me and knew he was right. I closed the business but I didn't completely let go. I keep these skills sharp, attending to them as regularly as I can, but as enrichments, not trades.

Beware that you don't squash the benefit of creativity by trying to monetize it. If you don't have the opportunity for capital, don't worry because that's not the only objective. Just remember the real fulfillment comes from creating, even if you're no good. And if you have to step away for a time, be sure to return. Keep yourself close to creative outlets.

Creative hobbies have one other benefit—built in therapy. Psychologist Mihaly Csikszentmihalyi studied "flow" (where individuals are deeply absorbed in their creative work). He showed that people experience psychological benefits and reduced stress when fully engaged in creative tasks. They have been shown to slow cognitive decline and increase serotonin.[30] Who couldn't use more of that?

The range of options for pharmaceutical help is vast today, and while I'm grateful for that technology, I worry about the ease and availability of it. If you could skip the prescription and pick up a knitting needle to achieve the same results, would you? We tend to lean on the easiest solution. Learning a new skill takes time and energy that many of us don't have. But medications lose efficacy. Hobbies don't. Once your body metabolizes a drug, it's gone, taking its desired effects with it. It's processed then discarded. You cannot discard a skill. Nor can you dismiss the increased tenacity, insight, and therapeutic benefits gained as you obtain and maintain it.

Your values and gifts define you more than anything or anyone else can. Define your core values, discover a hobby or two, then continue to feed them both.

CONFIDENCE

It stands to reason that a strong sense of identity will naturally evoke confidence. Confidence is the opposite of doubt and a herald of reason. But there are a couple problems with confidence.

While **confidence** can be an asset, no question, ask yourself, how important is it really? Is it more valuable than aptitude, passion, persistence? Would you trade it for clarity, direction, or support? It's difficult to ignore the proof that confidence is overrated. There are countless examples of public figures who struggle with confidence even in their celebrity and high performance. Research Abraham Lincoln, Mahatma Ghandi, Shaquille O'Neal, Serena Williams, Albert Einstein, and Simone Biles, and you'll find extremely high performing individuals who struggled with self-worth even at their productive peaks. Confidence is not as valuable as people assume. People can perform remarkably well without it. Confidence will wax and wane naturally, but the most enduring form of self-worth won't come from accomplishments, it will come from identity, growth, and balance.

Rather than replacing self-doubt with confidence, first look to **growth**. It's more measurable and sustainable. If you want to know your worth, to reach your potential, to make a difference, stay on an intentional course, one step at a time. If you focus on obtaining confidence, you'll end up surprisingly unsatisfied. Consider instead, what you may need to change about your identity and what you want to stay the same. And don't only think about your current self. Look ahead.

"We know what we are but not what we may be." [31]

Ophelia in Hamlet lamented the uncertainty of the future, but the gap between who we are now and who we can become is largely up to us, so much more than we realize. I offer the converse as well…

We know what we may be but forget who we are.

(If you're unfamiliar with the Rocky franchise, put the book down, take the day off, grab plenty of snacks and catch up. I promise it's worth your time. Plus, I'll refer to it repeatedly.)

Rocky Balboa is a bum. A "southpaw" from Philly, with no real talent except for grit and desire, he captures the hearts of millions with his rock-solid sense of self. He knows exactly who he is, and through six films spanning roughly thirty years, you can bet it's one of the film industry's most enduring examples of character consistency. As Rocky travels unfamiliar roads with exposure to varied cultural influences, we see him stretch and develop, but his innate identity persists. Through highs and lows, he remains the light-hearted, generous, simple-minded, loyal, Italian Stallion we fell for in the beginning.

We must maintain core, unbending parts of our identity, while embracing with flexibility our potential, to find the medium between these two extremes of identity crisis. Loving yourself *as you are,* is ground zero. Loving yourself *as you can* become, levels up from that foundation. They're not mutually exclusive. They're complimentary.

Current identity is the bedrock of all our dreams. So here's a solution to those disconnects—when it comes to who you are and who you can become, you—and only you—decide.

Next, consider **balance**. True self-worth doesn't come from achievement, it comes from balance. Imagine a table with four legs. When one leg is compromised, the whole table loses integrity. Pay attention to the four aspects of your life: physical, mental, social and spiritual. We often neglect one or two, or hone in on one in particular. The most grounded, sturdy table will have an equal balance of all four. Another benefit is that balance naturally diffuses perfectionism.

Being unbalanced confines you to a figurative box. Do you ever find yourself putting people into boxes? It's easy to slap on labels and judgements without much thinking. It takes effort to look deeply and honestly. But how often do we do this to ourselves? I cringe at the phrase, "I am who I am" when used as an excuse (that's usually the way it's used) because that's simply a refusal to grow. All the earth teaches us—if you're not changing, you're not living. Look a little deeper at those around you. Look with compassion and hope. Then apply that same treatment to yourself and step out of the box.

SUMMARY

Now the warning. Focus on self is only healthy as a means. What is the end? Any prolonged focus on self is potential poison, so let's put the emphasis of identity in its proper place. The objective of realizing your true identity is to maximize your contribution to the whole. Find the purpose of your individual existence and amplify that potential in order to make a positive difference in the world around you. That is the umbrella under which individuality should be served, the end that justifies the means.

By eliminating perfectionism, doubt, and comparison, you shed inaccurate assumptions of your identity. While you're at it, do away with labels, as well. We are all much more than a title, relationship, success, or mistake. By embracing your values and passions, you'll tap into your true potential. As you consider the aspects of your life that may need balance, continue to hone your character and individuality. Allow for flexibility and seek self-worth over confidence.

Write down at least three things that define you at your core, then list one way you can honor those traits today. Challenge any doubts about yourself, *for starters* are worth more than they know.

Success Hinges on Having the Right Team

"Alone we can do so little; together we can do so much."
Helen Keller

It takes a village. True or false?

There are two ends to this mental spectrum. Those at one end believe they can't move forward without "their people." They're hopeless without their tribe. At the other end, are those who believe that they are the master of their own fate and that no one else is needed. Which way do you lean?

When you tap into your true identity, that's where you'll find your power. But like our beloved electronic devices, your power is terribly limited without connection. It's the people around you who are the catalysts of that power. Like those coyotes in the desert, be so sure of who you are, that neither strangers *nor friends* can convince you otherwise. And be so sure of your team that you'll never be lost. You see, it's not about the village. It's about the team.

You have something unique to offer. Are the people around you maximizing it, or are they diminishing your potential? Is your team embracing or eliminating your identity? This is why we start with identity and then move right to your team. They need to be linked.

We naturally gravitate toward those who accept us as we are, but true growth comes from those who challenge us to reach our potential. You'll come across many people in your life and some will fan your flame while others snuff out your fire. Heed those who care less for your *present* comfort and more for your *eventual* fulfillment.

Consider again the "i" in "team." When it comes to our personal influencers, individual identity needs to be the foundation that you build the right team on.

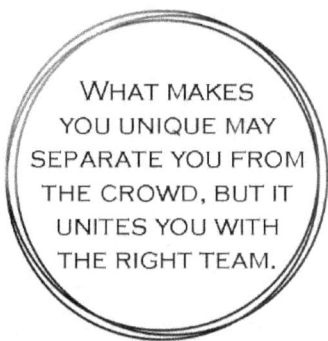

WHAT MAKES YOU UNIQUE MAY SEPARATE YOU FROM THE CROWD, BUT IT UNITES YOU WITH THE RIGHT TEAM.

"You are the average of the five people you spend the most time with."

Motivator Jim Rohn coined this widely accepted phrase that speaks to the power of influence. It speaks of your team. Our relationships are possibly the biggest contributing factor of who we can become in life. I've been schooled about teams from the day I was born. Not only from America's Team, "The Dallas Cowboys" as the daughter of their star quarterback, but in a tight-knit, traditional family, consisting of a loving mother, father, and three close brothers. Did my brothers rough my edges? Absolutely. Would they defend me in a heartbeat? I count on it.

These two environments, highlighted in the book Dad and I wrote, *Danny White: Spotlights & Shadows*, taught me loads about people and relationships, and how to scrutinize those that are beneficial and those that aren't. Since most of my lessons growing up were somehow related to, in preparation for, triggered by, or at least analogous to sports, I identified a fitting comparison to categorize the three most critical relationships. These associations help us achieve optimal balance and pave the way for success.

They are our ultimate influencers.

We need coaches. We need teammates. And we need fans.

No man is an island. We won't make it solo. There's a story in the QuRan about Noah, when he was on the ark, calling out to one of his sons who had decidedly not jumped aboard the ark. Noah called out for him to join, but the son chose to separate himself from the family and take his chances alone. *"I will betake myself to a mountain, it will save me from the water,"* was his response. But as the story goes, a wave came between them and he was drowned.[32]

The most important relationship you'll have is with God. The second is with yourself. All else you need is your team.

✓ Starters know their team

COACHES

A kite can't rise without its grounding string. If you haven't figured this out for yourself already, it's time you learn. You need a coach. Probably several. Having an objective and insightful leader does not show a lack of self-worth. Conversely, having someone to report to and glean from is a sign of success and intelligence. It's admitting, "I have room for improvement and I'm fully here for it." It's showing up for oneself, honing skills, and investing in becoming better. You'd be hard-pressed to find a successful person who *doesn't* have a mentor. It actually screams self-worth.

Good coaches are skilled trainers who have been where you've been and have the means to use that experience to assist you in your development. They share your enthusiasm, prepare you for what's to come, remind you of your training, allow you to learn the hard way when necessary, and jump in only when you need rescuing.

Penny Werthner, from the University of Calgary, interviewed 30 Olympic or Paralympic athletes and 27 coaches after the 2008 Olympic Games in Beijing, where Canada produced eighteen medals. She discovered five key factors shared by athletes who obtained a medal or a personal best. They consisted of the following:

- level of athlete self-awareness
- quality of the training environment
- management of the competitive environment
- support mechanisms
- coach-athlete relationship

What would you guess was the most influential factor in Olympic success? Coming in at number one, was the coach-athlete relationship.

A coach may or may not be an expert, but being at least a step or two ahead, provides help in vital ways: skills, motivation, accountability, strategic guidance, physical and mental conditioning, team cohesion and communication, performance analysis, constructive feedback, and personal development. Through the years, as my dad reminisced about the days he played for the Dallas Cowboys, one name prevailed above all others—Landry. There's no question that in his performance and development as an athlete, legendary coach Tom Landry played a critical role, and was by all accounts, head and shoulders above the rest.

If you reflect on some of your greatest achievements, is there an image of a mentor that comes to mind? Someone who challenged you because they believed in you?

A good coach will:
- Cut you down. They're not afraid to hurt you to build you. If you're tough enough to take it and stay, they'll build you back up. That's the process of growth.

- Allow you to ruminate and discover problems for yourself.
- Spare lectures and negotiations. You can count on their follow through, positive and negative.
- Reward effort over achievement. They'll measure success by progress rather than performance.
- Pull—not push—from you all the best you have to offer. They don't preach, they engage. They see, they listen, they don't talk too much. They instruct and motivate, and then they shut up.
- Demonstrate their expertise when necessary, but allow you to take the front stage.
- Balance critique and praise to the point you know they've got your back when it matters.
- Shines the light on your fears so you can take control of them, and at critical points move in close.
- Match your efforts, and campaign for you shamelessly.
- Damage your pride, and that's the point. After talking you through it, they'll show you an increase of love and support.
- Play the long game. Match their patience.

The best coaches are not afraid to stretch the truth either. Josie was by far the leading rebounder for her basketball team. At half time during a close and intense game, her coach screamed at her, "Jos, you only have *three* rebounds! I need you to step it up!!" In the second half, she pulled down seven more boards before fouling out, in her best effort to appease her coach and help her team. Come to find out, she actually had nine rebounds at the half and ended the game with a personal record of 16 rebounds in a game. *Lie* is a strong word, but a coach will absolutely let you *believe wrong...* when it benefits the team.

When searching for a mentor, find someone who aligns with your ideas and connects with you where you are but sees you for what you can become. Someone who has wisdom to offer. You're not looking for a buddy or someone who makes you feel good about yourself—that's another role.

Two basketball icons who worked together for ten seasons and won three consecutive NBA championships were Kobe Bryant and Phil Jackson. Kobe said of his coach, *"He's like a Zen Master. He has a great balance of intuition and analytics. He knows exactly when to push my buttons and when not to."*

The impact a coach can have is only part of the equation. The **coachability** of the subject makes up the rest. There are several traits a coachable individual will possess, which are fairly common knowledge—characteristics like accountability, work ethic, IQ, EQ, ability. But there is a subtler checklist that separates the good from the *better* students.

When checking yourself for coachability add these two traits. Master them and a good coach will work wonders with you:

- **Willingness**. Show a coach you trust them. Show them a determined desire to let them guide you without question. Like when Mick makes Rocky chase the chickens in Rocky I. The task seemed ridiculous at the time, but a coach has perspective. Trust that wisdom and trust the process. Willingness trumps ability. A good coach will take heart over aptitude every time.
- **Humility**. So much is wrapped up in this one little word. Humility implies ownership—a key ingredient in coachability. It implies confidence, not the cocky kind of confidence that inflates ego, but the balanced confidence that comes from a true sense of identity—knowing what one is able to contribute to the team. Humility

worries less about hierarchy and more about harmony. There is no jealousy or comparison, only a desire to improve what's been given, to make a contribution.

I was sitting next to a speaking coach after he'd given me feedback about a presentation I just finished. He kept leaning over to me, positively analyzing the speaker who was following me. He kept highlighting all the things she was doing well after he'd given me a couple suggestions of things I could improve on. Pridefully, I took all his compliments to her as digs toward me. We do this too often and it is a sure sign of pride.

Coachable is neither combative nor offendable. When instruction is given, there should be no argument or push-back. A good coach will see insecurity as the poison of pride it is. One man's success is not another's failure. Learn to take critiques as opportunities to improve. Take them as a compliment that someone sees enough potential in you to care. And never take the success of others personally.

Time is a precious commodity. You have no control of how much you get, only how you use it. So ask yourself who you are giving airtime to. Who are you allowing to be your influencers? I'm amazed at the amount of advice we accept from celebrities and public figures simply because they have the mic. Money, publicity, or a cool British accent are not qualifiers for expertise. And a "following" is a qualifier for nothing except how to gain followers.

A word about intuition. Intuition can be a coach itself. When coaching parents regarding their children, I reserve the right to be wrong, because parental intuition is not to be argued with. One thing better than good advice is God's advice. Don't discard your intuition or that of your best coaches for less qualifying intel.

Who has your best interest? Are you listening to them?

Who are you listening to? Do they have your best interest?

TEAMMATES

✓ Starters put the team goal first

While coaches provide the best guidance, teammates are at your side, ready to help you implement. This is my favorite of the three relationships to discuss because it has the potential to be the most productive. It can also be the most difficult. We love our friends. We want them all to be good teammates, but the ugly truth of it is… they may not be. Examination of your teammates is eye-opening.

As Jim Rohn suggested, we tend to become like the people closest to us. That influence of our environment is the reason we develop accents and learn behaviors. In this friend zone, nature is often battling nurture and losing. It's wise to be careful who we surround ourselves with.

———— • • ————

My dad had a pilot's license and a little Beechcraft Baron private plane that he adored. One regular trip he liked to make was from our home in McKinney, Texas to see family in Mesa, Arizona. It was typically a smooth flight except for a brief passage above a mountain range in New Mexico where the ride could get a little bumpy from unstable air. The Baron was unpressurized, so he had to keep it under 18,000 feet.

One particular trip, we had the whole family in tow. As expected, turbulence showed up over New Mexico, but Dad thought nothing of it. He knew this route, he was an experienced pilot, all was well, ETA one hour. Mom, however, dialed into a different destination as a storm materialized over the mountains. The turbulence worsened. My brothers and I were getting fussy and mom started to panic. With less than an hour to go, all Dad wanted was to ride out the storm and get to his destination. But our mom chose her battles, and she was not going to lose this one. She demanded he turn the plane around and put it down at the closest airport, Socorro.

In the middle of that stormy night, we safely touched down in Socorro, NM. But in those late hours and with a convention in town, rooms were scarce. The family had a most inconvenient night in the harbor of a police station lobby, but Dad didn't complain.

I'll never know what the outcome would have been had he disregarded his partner's demands. I'm thankful for that. I'm thankful for the trust they showed in one another all their lives. When Mom was finishing her fight with cancer, she looked to Dad for guidance. She wanted to keep fighting but we knew she needed to let Heaven take over. Even in the end, she trusted him to make the hardest decision of his life, letting her go.

The thing about teammates is, it's not the person so much as the alignment. It's critical that the ultimate goal and focus are in sync. A true teammate loses individuality in sight of the common goal and is willing to make personal sacrifices. That is how synergy is born.

Here are some hallmarks of a good teammate:
- They put the team first, even when it's harder on them. They support the whole and recognize that as top priority.
- They build. They're constructive, not destructive. They choose compliments over critiques and don't complain unless offering a solution.
- They challenge you. They're competitive in healthy ways, leveraging your weaknesses and amplifying your strengths.
- Like a coach, they're not afraid to hurt your feelings when it's what you need, so toughen up.
- They show no jealousy. You'll recognize them by

their focus—it'll never be on themself.

True teammates are on the same playing field. No one is above the other, they are equals. When you find someone who cares more about *what's best* for you than what he/she wants, whose efforts are outward, not inward, you've found a teammate.

———— • ————

Mariano Rivera, Hall of Fame pitcher for the Yankees, lost the 2001 world series in game seven to the Diamondbacks. The loss was unexpected and an especially devastating blow to Rivera, who allowed the winning run.

During this championship, Rivera's friend and teammate, Enrique Wilson, was confident his team would win game seven and scheduled his travel back home to the Dominican Republic to allow time for post-game celebrations in New York.

When his team lost, he decided to change his flight and head home earlier. His original flight 587 from JFK never made it to the Dominican Republic. It crashed shortly after departure and all passengers plus several civilians on the ground were killed.

At spring training the following year, Mariano Rivera said something I doubt anyone else has said. "I'm glad we lost the world series." A game seven win would have kept Wilson on flight 587, ending both his career and his life. Rivera explained what mattered more than game seven, "I still have my friend."

Rivera won five World Series, one more after this loss. Enrique Wilson never won the fall classic, but he won a lifelong teammate.

———— • ————

There was a time I got in serious trouble, but Mom was too busy to follow through with her usual discipline—time alone in my room followed by a formal spanking. Not wanting to break routine, she informed me she was putting her partner on it. She was sending Dad. Sitting in probation, I was more than anxious as

I stewed on all the possibilities. I fixated on that bedroom door, waiting, not knowing what to expect.

When he entered, he looked defeated, as if an inner turmoil was brewing. I sat petrified, wanting neither to accelerate nor postpone whatever was about to happen. He sat next to me on the bed and said, "Mom sent me in here to give you a spanking, you know."

Yes, I sure did know, but the words wouldn't form so I offered a slow nod.

"You know what you did wrong?"

Yes, I sure did. Again, just a nod.

"Will you just promise me to not do it again?"

Yes, I sure would. Was I about to get out of this unscathed? Our matching brown eyes met, and I knew he couldn't follow through. He was taking the role of teammate. The coach had done her job, and he knew what I needed at that moment was an equal, a partner.

Kelly and I have been married a long time, more than half my life now. He and I have been teammates on a variety of ventures and there have been times when we were not very good ones. (If you want to test your marriage...become business partners.) When those difficult times come, we have to apply three actions: connect, communicate, and champion. Realigning puts us back on track to being good teammates.

Connect. A friend of mine, Julie DeJesus, shares a compelling keynote presentation about the importance of connection. Her hallmark phrase is, "Happiness is not our business. Connection is." Find common ground. If you can't connect, you can't team.

Communicate. Too many conflicts originate from poor communication. Learn to be fully present, humble, and understanding. Be clear, patient, and respectful. Remember the wise words of behaviorist Thomas Erikson, *"Communication happens on the listener's terms."*

Champion is both a noun and a verb, but I'm afraid it's most commonly used for its lesser productive variation. Only the verb form of the word matters here, denoting the action of a person who fights for a cause or argues on behalf of someone else. Teammates champion one another.

When I meet with a new group or organization, I can gauge the health of their team/s quickly by observing one thing—interactions. Where they're positive, openly engaged and complimentary, I know they're lifting one another and unity will be easy. Where they're slow to interact, protective, and segregated, I see we've got some work to do.

Teammates make you better by accelerating your progress. They see successes as *ours* and failures as *ours,* no matter what. There's no blame, shame, jealousy, or comparison. Teammates pick up after each other and they pick each other up.

Look at the past year of your life. Have you accomplished all you set out to? If not, check your teammates.

If you *know* better than you *do*, check your teammates.

If you get inspired about making a change, then feel something pulling you back, check your teammates.

If you're not sure how to check your teammates, ask your coach.

FANS

I've heard suggestions that the analogy ends here. That in the walk of life it's really only necessary to have someone in front of you and someone at your side. That coaches and teammates matter, but a cheering section, while desirable, doesn't really make a difference. What do you say?

Whether fans are absolutely necessary is debatable, but the fact that fans make a difference is irrefutable.

When I work with teams, I ask them to visualize a bad morning.

Try it. We all have them so it's not much of a stretch—imagine one of those days you wake up and can't find your inner-starter. You try to talk to God but He's not answering. No new messages on your phone. You go to the mirror, and it is just not your day. All you see staring back at you is a nobody, a worthless loser who should do the world a favor and go back to bed.

Concluding that life stinks and the sun doesn't shine, imagine yourself giving in to the woes and heading back to bed. But as you get there, you find an envelope on the pillow. On the front is your first name, nothing else. You open it and begin to read a handwritten letter addressed to you. It is affectionate and personal, as the writer begins listing all the incredible things about you. Obviously written by someone who knows you well, the letter details all your strengths and highlights your unique abilities. It lists all the good that you are and makes you feel like a superstar. There's no advice, no "feedback." It simply goes on and on with compliments of all the good things you are. And within moments, you know your potential. You have something to offer, and you're ready to get started.

Who wrote the letter? Did that person make a difference?

Self-esteem isn't reliable and self-confidence tends to wane. Both are subject to comparison, which is never healthy. Having someone who loves you for no reason gives you wings. Not having to worry about your value being contingent on your performance—that's freeing.

When life gets scary, and it will, you'll need to know who is cheering you on, even (and especially) if you're doing something sketchy, risky, or plain stupid.

True, we need checks and balances, people to warn us when we're about to jump off a cliff. That's what coaches and teammates are for. But who's going to applaud the jump? Because we need those people too.

There would be a lot of influential people without a job and without influence, were it not for fans. And when it comes to performance, we'll do things for a fan we wouldn't for a coach.

Most people have never heard of Christopher Little. He was a struggling literary agent in London who saw incredible potential in an unlikely candidate. After reading a few chapters of a brand-new unpublished author's work, he was captivated. He decided to take a chance and began to advocate for her. He sent the book out to his network of publishers. Twelve of them sent him rejection letters, but he refused to be defeated and continued to *champion* this young author.

Finally, he was able to convince someone to publish the book for a meager price. Not what he and the author had hoped for, but it was a start. The book was *Harry Potter.*

Being a fan takes such little effort and has an incredible potential for reward. The point of Christopher Little's story is not what it did for *his* career in the end (estimated £60 million) but what it did for the young author, J.K. Rowling, a now household name who has influenced countless lives with her inspirational creation. Did he make a difference?

When Rowling was looking for an agent to sell her book, she was looking for a teammate, maybe even a coach. But while you can attempt to choose your coaches and teammates, you can't choose your fans. By traditional standards of value, that significantly increases their worth.

———————— • ————————

When our daughter Tess was eight, she participated in her first singing recital. Since her infancy, people noticed her unique, deep, raspy voice. With an added ability to identify and match pitch perfectly, we put her in music lessons to harness the instrument. I grew up going to musicals and spending plenty of time in theater auditoriums, so I knew the etiquette. My husband and son however, did not have the same background. They were more used to sporting events. So when we arrived in the massive auditorium for her recital I had to quickly and quietly give them a crash course in what was and wasn't appropriate behavior.

Tess had two numbers, back-to-back. This was her first time on a big stage with the towering red velvet curtains and bright spotlights on her. She timidly shuffled up to the mic, and that spacious, dark auditorium seemed to swallow her up. I could feel her nerves from my seat. She started out softly and a couple lines in, lost her way. She forgot the words and froze. After about five seconds, that felt like minutes, she found her way back on track. As if nothing happened, she locked in on all she'd practiced and finished strong. Her second song was her favorite. She confidently boomed it out, filling the entire room with her sweet smoky voice and energetic personality. She absolutely killed it.

As the heavy applause was beginning to die down her 18-yr-old brother who must not have been paying attention to my lecture, shouted out, "Obvious winner!"

Um. There are no winners at a music recital. Part of me was mortified. The rest of me was bursting with gratitude for the bond they shared and the honor he felt being on her team.

Fans cheer for you even when they don't fully understand what you're doing. They're not there for the game, they're there for you. They not only see you, they accept you. That acceptance removes judgment. It bridges any generational, cultural, or hierarchical gaps that may be inhibiting a connection. When someone shows that they not only see and understand you, but that they appreciate you as you are, that's a fan.

Living with a celebrity taught me to be a skeptic. My father didn't act differently because he was a celebrity. The only difference his celebrity made was the way people acted around *us*. There are many different kinds of fans, from fair-weather to true. Beware of bought fans, the follow-for-follows on social media, members of a cohort who feel an obligation or who stand to benefit from your success. Fans aren't about alignment or affiliation. They run deeper than that. It's not their counsel that binds you to them, it's their lack of conditions. Real fans show up uninvited. They have a funny memory, sharp with your wins, and hazy with your losses. They purchase your product behind your back at full price. True fans are invested with no promise of return. Their celebration of you is unending. And when you do win, they're not surprised, they're validated.

I know what you may be thinking. *I don't have fans.* First, you're wrong. You're not looking in the right places. Second, the best way to gain fans is to become one. There are days we'll lose faith in humanity. When it seems most people are only looking out for themselves. Too often it feels true because it is true. Most people, most of the time, do what's best for themselves. Fact of life. But here's a fact of Heaven—you have a gazillion fans. They are cheering you on from beyond this world. A favorite Bible story of mine tells of the prophet Elisha's small Israelite army when they faced the vast Syrians. His servant saw only the disproportionate opposition but the prophet saw the host of heavenly fans. Did that angelic army make a difference?

And so we return to the question we started with. Can you succeed without fans? Let me ask you this. Will it feel like success if you're all alone? Your fans are your tribe. And most often the truest fans will come from those already on your team—your coaches and teammates.

EXPECTATIONS

Once you've found your true team, a warning about **expectations**. You have no control over how someone shows up in your life. There will be times you find yourself labeling someone as a potential coach, teammate, or fan, and setting expectations for them. That gets dangerous. Unless you are a boss with employees or a parent of young children, you have no business putting expectations on anyone else, especially without their consent. You control you.

We all have that one flaky friend. Why do we keep them around?

Because they likely occupy a role like coach or fan, but when we try to make them a teammate, they fall short. But that's on us for expecting them to fill a role they're not fit for.

We're made up of pieces. So are our relationships. When someone doesn't give the way you want them to, you can choose to accept them in parts, however small those parts may be. Don't discount someone for not occupying a space, when they fittingly occupy another. Graciously take what your influencers give, and dismiss where they fall short.

Successfully building a team will ensure one thing: opponents. Sometimes they're loud and obnoxious. The more dangerous ones are unseen, insidiously living inside your head. But just like any obstacle, they can be used for your benefit. Opponents are opportunities.

There is an inspiring book about the genius of Abraham Lincoln filling his presidential cabinet with his former opponents and critics. He doesn't change their views or defeat their cause; he wins them over with a stronger alignment. Finding common ground in commitment to the Union and abolition of slavery. He sees the good they have to offer and capitalizes on that. From *Team of Rivals: The Political Genius of Abraham Lincoln...*

> *"This, then, is a story of Lincoln's political genius revealed*
> *through his extraordinary array of personal qualities*
> *that enabled him to form friendships with men who*
> *had previously opposed him; to repair injured*
> *feelings that, left untended, might have*
> *escalated into permanent hostility."*
> Doris Kearns Goodwin[33]

Choosing to dismiss a person too hastily can be both immature and unwise. Don't define others by their stance or affiliation. Lean in. Where possible, find something to admire and something to glean. Accept the respectable pieces of people you dislike and

61

teach those in your circle to do the same.

———————• •———————

In 2022, 30% of households in the United States were non-family households (meaning persons in that home were unrelated to anyone else by birth, marriage, or adoption). That number is double what it was in 1970. In 2024, 29% of households were single person households, which is up 19% from 1974. Currently, about 46% of U.S. adults are single.[34]

We're trending away from family, but it is in our homes we often find both our toughest critics and our biggest fans. We would be remiss if we didn't use those relationships to our advantage. Rather than expecting more from them, maximize the contributions of your personal team by slotting them into their respective roles and applying all they offer to your growth.

- Trust your coach enough to implement all the things they've given you to implement. Act on their advice.
- Be vulnerable with your teammates. Allow them to understand how you're feeling and where you're coming from. Expose them to your weaknesses *and* your strengths so you can achieve the synergy you're meant for.
- For your fans, be the person they think you are. Show them a recovery. There's nothing fans love more than watching their hero rise after a fall.

When someone in your life can occupy any three of these roles, depending on what you need at the time, hang on to them tight! Value them for the rare gift they are and do your best to reciprocate. I've told Kelly more than a time or two, "Right now I need a fan, not a coach." It's marital communication gold.

There are some similarities and overlap among the roles. As

62

mentioned, teammates can make great fans. Some attributes they all share:

- They are all your advocates.
- They all see your potential and value progress over perfection.
- They all show up.
- They will all champion you by promoting, defending, and upholding you—spin new meaning on the word *championship*.

SUMMARY

You have something special to offer. Is your team supporting it? In business, you'll have investors, partners, and customers. In health—doctors, nurses, and coaches. In education—teachers, classmates. All around you are influencers. When you need help, who do you call? When you need brutal honesty, advice, direction, a hand, a shoulder? Your coaches, teammates, and fans. It doesn't take a village. It takes a team.

Note a key difference in the three roles, namely proximity and perspective.

Fans aren't always aware of the intricacies of your situation. They're just there for you, rain or shine, win or lose, cheering you on. They see through rose-colored glasses and have total faith in all you can do.

Coaches are a step closer. The best coaches genuinely see what you're going through. They know where you've been and hold tremendous insight with that perspective. Respect it and take their advice above all else. They know what it takes.

Teammates are in the trenches with you. They know your situation intimately, although they may have a different investment or challenge. Though they are at your side, their perspective is not exactly the same. Trust their eyes when they see something you don't. The bonds you make with your teammates will be lasting.

Can you see the immeasurable value of each of these perspectives? Which one do you need most in your life right now? These three critical relationships impact our identity, our goals, and our productivity more than any other relationships. Write the names of the five people you spend the most time with. Are they a coach, teammate, or fan? What adjustments could you make to your current team? Trust that the impact on your life will be worth it.

You chase the dream because of a coach.

You work the dream because of a teammate.

You succeed because of fans.

If you want to build yourself the optimal climate for success, you'll surround yourself with these three types of people. Opponents are a sign you built a good team. Critics will show up uninvited, especially if you're on the right track, so don't let that discourage you. Let it toughen and humble you.

Coaches, teammates, and fans are *for starters.*

Impact Is Only Achieved Through Action

"The value of an idea lies in the using of it."
Thomas Edison

Not in an idea's origin, its potential, or its creativity, but in its execution. Good intentions get you no points here. The credit belongs to the man actually in the arena.[35]

Many people are grateful, sure of their identity and sure of their team. What separates the starters is movement. I hope you noticed that the first three principles are intrinsic and internal. They support who you are as an individual. The last three principles are about what you *do* with that individuality.

The very word *productive* denotes action. If you imagine pushing a heavy concrete ball, what would be the most difficult part of that journey? Starting. Once the ball is rolling, it's about maintenance. When building campfires, I can easily pinpoint the moment when I have the most anxiety. It is when I breathlessly place the new flame into the structure I've created. Not necessarily when I light the match, but when I take that ignition to the next level. That is when I am going to find out if my preparation was adequate—the test that will determine whether I have succeeded or failed.

> *"When you come to the edge of all the light and knowledge you have and take a step into the darkness of the unknown you must believe one of two things will happen. There will be something solid for you to stand on, or you will be taught how to fly."*
> *Patrick Overton*

This quote prominently hung in my home growing up. It was etched on a metal plate, attached to a framed photograph of an eagle. It's inspirational for me, but throughout my coaching I've come to realize many people are not quite ready to spread their wings. Some won't take that step because they lack conviction in either themselves, a system, divinity, or humanity. For them, this quote isn't inspiring at all. It's terrifying.

What if you're not ready to take that step into the darkness? What if you are uncertain that you'll have the resources to fly? Several factors affect our ability to get started and find momentum. Often, we need help finding that impetus. We have the *desire* for a thriving new business, a diploma, a clean house, or a waistline, but we can't seem to pull the trigger.

If you find yourself struggling to act, it may be a sign of inadequate self-worth. Another reason why identity must be examined.

Do you find your personality swaying with your circumstances and environment? Do you find yourself frustrated or happy, relative to where you are, who you're with, or what you're doing? If the defining qualities of your identity are still in question, we'll address a critical key in this chapter that has a little less to do with what you're made of and more to do with what you make.

Productivity is realized when there is alignment between who you are and what you're doing. We cannot **become** what we're meant to become without a matching **action**. And without knowing who we are, we won't be able to act.

- In the notorious program of Alcoholics Anonymous, there are twelve *steps* to *becoming* sober. Action helps us to become.
- In countless professions, we must be *qualified* before we can perform. Becoming helps us with action.

Action and identity support one another—you cannot sustain one without the other. Assuming you've got a handle on who you are, we must explore how to light that fire. The three pillars of action are Cause, Control, and Discomfort.

CAUSE

Besides an aligned identity and outside influence (a team) when needed, it's common to think the only two things you need to get started are:

1. Ability
2. Opportunity

Those are necessary, yes, but there's one other helpful prerequisite. It's what stalls or propels us when we're looking into that unknown darkness. The third factor that makes all the difference between taking that leap and staying where we are is our **cause**. It stems from our identity's *reason*. It's the lit match we're going to use to start our fire. Ability and opportunity are critical, but even with an abundance of both, it's never been easier to do nothing. With so much mindless information at our fingertips it's too easy to procrastinate and waste time. So we stay put, until a new purpose motivates us to move.

> *"Sometimes our pain pushes us,*
> *and sometimes our hope pulls us."*
> Dr. Edith Eva Eger

Would you jump into a frozen lake for no reason? Probably not. But if your friend was drowning in it, would you even hesitate? What would you do to save a child? To cure a disease? A cause is the most effective impetus you can have because it gives you something to lose.

I love hearing true American Dream success stories. They tend to begin the same—with a figurative back against a wall. Layoffs, poor prognoses, or other unfortunate events force people to do things they otherwise wouldn't. Living on a prayer, they must make some rash and hopeful decisions because of compelling causes like bills to pay, families to feed, and lives to save. You don't see people with predictably stable finances taking the same financial risks as those without... because they lack cause. Given the right cause, the edge of that cliff is no contest.

Whenever I had an art commission, I promised my client a deadline. That deadline was more for me than them. Without it, I'd get distracted, and it would lose priority. That date became my cause, my reason to keep up. If the deadline approached and I wasn't wrapping up, I'd create another reason by bringing my project out of the studio and onto the kitchen table. Putting it in our central location gave me lots of reasons and incentive to finish.

Your cause doesn't have to be profound. It could simply be... you've started. It's hard to give up skydiving if you've already jumped out of the plane.

Once you have your reason, make a plan, don't overthink it. If your objective is clear and your cause is pure, the odds are already in your favor. When we think too much, we psych ourselves out. Yes, planning is important, but it does us no good unless at some point you take the leap. Might as well be when you're excited about it.

Hope is "more than the sunny view that everything will turn out all right"; it is "believing you have the will and the way to accomplish your goals."
Daniel Goleman

Mr. Goleman shares my belief in a more productive *hope.* Rather than a complacent wishing, it is an active, intentional reaching. Ability, opportunity, and a cause, that's what you need to start a fire. Now how to keep it lit.

✓ Starters don't stop moving

I learned a difficult lesson with a Rolex that had its movement stolen by a shady jeweler. It's the movement that matters. Even if it's in the wrong direction, a habit of always moving will make sure you avoid indifference. Indifference and apathy are dreaded chains, much worse than occasional course corrections. An addiction recovery facilitator once told me that most of the members in his group were on step 36 of the twelve-step program. And I said, hooray!

Action closes the gap between plan and production. When sighting in a shooting device, like a bow or a gun, it's impossible to gain accuracy without firing. You must pull the trigger. Only then can you ascertain precision, make adjustments and repeat until aim is reliable. When my clients are stuck on a difficult decision, I help them identify the goal and the cause (even if just sketches). Together we pick one thing, no matter how small, to *do* and one thing to *not do* in support of the goal. As soon as they start moving, often they want to make small adjustments to the goal. It's *action* that dispels uncertainty and helps to define the goal.

Malcolm Gladwell's *Outliers* popularized the theory that it takes 10,000 hours to master a skill. If you don't move, it won't take long before you lose the ground you've gained. All your preparation and steps you've taken will start to disintegrate. Paralysis, anxiety, fear—though we can not control their onset, we must be willing to confront them. Like pushing the big concrete ball, don't lose momentum or it'll be difficult to get it going again. One step at a time. Just keep stepping.

IMPEDIMENTS

A fact of business: most startups fail. Lack of persistence is primarily the culprit of that failure—but starters don't accept failure.

So, what stalls action? Fear, distraction, and discouragement are at the top of the list. But there are tricks to overcoming them, so you're not doomed.

Fear. Merriam Webster defines it as "an unpleasant, often strong emotion caused by anticipation or awareness of danger."[36] An emotion. This means it only exists for the person experiencing it, which means it could potentially... not exist. Train your mind to lean in and examine your fears. According to fear expert Gavin De Becker, *"Linking an unwarranted fear to its ultimate terrible destination usually helps alleviate that fear."*[37]

While fear can be an impetus it can also be an impediment. In subtler forms, fear can look like uncertainty or worry. All elicit avoidance—action's nemesis.

Fear, as a response to a threat, is designed to keep us safe. Here's the science in a nutshell. Our senses perceive a threat and create glutamate which travels to the hypothalamus. A signal is then sent to our glands to create adrenaline and consequently a number of physical reactions we have no control over—increased heart rate, sweating, trembling, running and screaming, you get the picture. In short, our body reacts automatically to a perceived threat. I haven't heard of anyone yet who can control the creation of glutamate in their body unfortunately.

Fear is important when it keeps us safe. There are certainly benefits to fear. But when it comes to productivity, you must make sure your relationship with it is healthy and your cause is fueled by something more reliable.

Do you get caught over-planning before acting and implementing? Do you procrastinate, overthink, or stall? These can be detrimental. Quickly moving on a good idea or prompting can give you just the edge you need. Have you ever been worried about investing in a door that might end up closing on you? Worry is a type of fear worth mentioning here because it keeps us from starting. As soon as you get an inkling that the benefit is potentially greater than the risk, you have to act fast.

If you're worried about failure, meditate on this. Mistakes are just like closed doors. They have tremendous value—often as much as success and open doors. A closed door eliminates a wrong path, so it's okay if you make some bad turns.

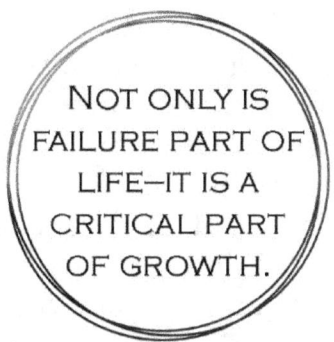

NOT ONLY IS FAILURE PART OF LIFE—IT IS A CRITICAL PART OF GROWTH.

Owning your choices also means owning your mistakes. Decide to say oops and ask yourself, "What's to be learned?" Failure is a commendable teacher. Dr. Carol Dweck, American psychologist at Stanford University, is renowned for her expertise in motivation and mindset. She states, "In the fixed mindset, everything is about the outcome. If you fail—or if you're not the best—it's all been wasted. The growth mindset allows people to value what they're doing *regardless of the outcome.*" If you dismiss or disown your mistakes too quickly, you'll miss vital opportunities for growth. Learn how to take fear by the throat and show it who's boss.

✓ Starters own their mistakes

When fear causes you to start, it's unreliable. When it causes you to *not* start, it's potentially damning. Don't look for reasons to wait. Look forward to the lessons you'll get from both the wins and the losses. Don't push your fears aside. If you bury or ignore them, they'll pop back up. But don't bow down to them either. Give them the attention they seek, not the control they seek. Addressing fears honestly and humbly is the best way to know if they are serving you well. Because sometimes they do.

Distraction is a rampant obstacle these days, and we're all plagued by it. Distraction can increase cognitive overload, stress, and anxiety. It diminishes creativity and can even affect relationships. Too much focus on self can be a distraction. Some remedies to distraction include time-blocking, organization, and adjusting your environment. But you won't find a remedy that doesn't involve action.

Discouragement is on the other end of the scale from confidence. But the opposite of discouragement gives yet another trait that supersedes confidence in value—courage. Courage is handy when you're lighting the fire and courage continues to fan the flame. It will take you further than confidence ever could.

CONTROL

Now a shortcut. There is actually one principle that abates all barriers to action—the trick that combats all impediments. Control.

Starters win with grace and dignity. They win as a team and share the praise they receive with those who helped them get there. But one reason they know how to win so well is because they have learned how to lose well.

———— • ————

Kelly is a real fan for several pro teams, and he takes their losses hard. Often, when his team loses he'll receive gloating messages from his friends or acquaintances and it really gets to him. He's learned to walk away from his phone or computer when his teams take a big L. One year, after his team was beaten out of the NFC Championship by a rival, he was especially down. That's why I was surprised to see the next morning on social media, Kelly's message to his cousin, "Congrats, cousin. They sure know how to win!" His cousin's favorite team is the one Kelly detests most. But he loves his cousin more. He didn't have to say anything. No one would have cared. But swallowing his hurt and reaching out to cheer for his cousin helped him recover. This is another benefit of being a fan—cheering eases pain—for all parties.

Kelly perfectly illustrated the unification of *being* and *doing* as he illustrated control, the most important principle of action.

Once you recognize what's holding you back, you begin to take control. Being led by your cause will either steer you away from something or toward something. It really doesn't matter what gets you moving but running from a lion (fear), though a compelling reason, doesn't specify a direction. When you're moving, make sure you have something in your sights. *Reaching for* is more sustainable than *running from* because it turns reaction to action.

✓ Starters don't react, they act

That can feel like splitting hairs because we're often motivated to act by a situation or event. The way we split the hairs is with control. Action is voluntary, reaction is involuntary. When you are in control, that's action.

Take fear for example. Understanding that fear, like doubt, only exists in your head is only step one. Next you must handle it with control. To begin taking control of (or at least mitigate) fear, a person has to first ascertain the threat. What is it that's worrying you?

There are two options for controlling a threat: Change your perception of it, or remove it.

What's the potential harm? Identify the threat your brain is trying to protect you from and whether it really exists. Pick it apart. Lean in. If control is out of your hands, decide then what aspects you *can* control.

The best way to remove yourself from a threatening situation is to not be there in the first place. If the situation can be manipulated in a way that neutralizes the threat, say goodbye to fear. Be sharp at noticing and heeding the signs all around that warn of threats. Some are obvious. "Don't feed the crocodiles." Subtler signs can include advice from loved ones or friends who've been bitten. Teams are so handy.

The reverse effect of control is seen with addiction. At some point, your drug of choice changes from seeking pleasure to avoiding pain, surrendering to addiction. At first, you were running toward something, but you ended up being chased by a lion.

———————— • • ————————

One strategy for taking control is making sure you're operating in the present time. My favorite coach in sports was a high school volleyball coach, Mel Fuchigami. He was an older, larger, Polynesian guy who thought he spoke better English than he really did. He was tough, brutal actually, but I warmed up to him right away. One day after an emotionally difficult day at school, I went to practice depressed, and he noticed. During warmups he took me aside. We sat on the gym floor, face to face over in a corner. "What matter?" he began.

I blubbered out my sixteen-year-old woes, while he sat staring at me. I never paused for questions or validation, didn't wait for any responses, just rambled on in all my teenage feels. Wrapping up, I stared back at him, waiting for his Miyagi-esque wisdom. After several silent seconds he brought a hand up to his eyebrows and pulled at the unruly hairs that shaded his eyes. He stretched them out so I could see how long they were. It was impressive, honestly. A good inch and a half at full reach. Finally, with his eyebrow hairs still extended, he spoke, "See this?"

I awkwardly nodded.

"Wife have to trim."

Okay... I thought. What does that have to do with... What the heck is happening here? He tipped over onto his hip and struggled his way up to his feet, then lent me a hand and pulled me up next to him. The conversation was over, and we got to work.

That experience puzzled me for a while, but I realize now what he was doing. He was bringing me into the present. My emotions were chained by both the past and the future. He made *now* my reality. Then over the next three hours he made my *now* so intense I couldn't stress about what had happened or worry about what might happen.

The most critical time when it comes to productivity is the **present**. You have no control outside of the present. Sure, you can influence the future, just as the past influences you now, but that's not control. We tend to let ourselves be paralyzed by the future or enslaved by the past. It's not their time. Set your sights on a goal but realize the current movement is what matters most, not what's behind you or ahead of you.

Three things you can control:
- Your actions. Here's a simple test. Are you acting or reacting? If the latter, you're not in control. Keep your actions intentional, as many as you possibly can, and they will be so much more productive.
- Your environment. Sometimes you're in an environment that makes control difficult. It's true, we are subjects of our environment but most of the time, if you think about it, your environment is something you can control. Keep yourself in the right places.
- Your opinions. That's right, you are under no obligation to share opinions or ideas with anyone, so choose your own buy-ins. A class they should teach in school is *How to Disagree Amicably*. Diversity makes the world go round.

81

When you base your worth on someone else's perception of you, who's in control? When your phone pings with a notification, are you in control when you check it? When society tells you you must do something a certain way, who decides if they're right?

Recognizing your control can affect so many aspects of your life. When I was approached by a solicitor after realizing this concept of control—that was life altering! The conversation wasn't defensive, I wasn't stressed about buying something I didn't want. I wasn't worried about anything really. I was holding all the cards, and it was empowering. Here's the point—I guarantee you're not taking advantage of all within your power.

———— • ————

The productive way to embrace what you can control is to first recognize and eliminate what you can't. For example, every new parent finds out real quick they have little to no control of their kids. They can control consequences and environments—and they should—but their kids' actions and emotions are totally out of parental hands.

Parents, what you *can do* is teach them the concept of control. Adopt this phrase, "*You control you.*" When sister whines about brother making her cry, *you control you, sis.* When the teacher didn't tell them the assignment was due, when they're unprepared, or late, or bothered, or stressed... *You control you.*

As the blessed only daughter among three sons, I often got into situations by affiliation that wouldn't normally have come my way. One such day, the four of us were out enjoying our summer freedom when my brothers got a great idea. We had a sport-court at our house growing up and spent a lot of time *not* playing the intended sports on it. Riding our bikes and skateboards was the activity of this particular day.

Geoff was propped up on his bike, one leg on the pedal, one on the ground. His neck was turned around, as if he were overseeing the proper set-up of the experiment. Ryan, the designated executioner, was carefully tying a rope from the back frame of the bike to a skateboard. Then he carefully, gently, centered me, his little sister, belly-down on the skateboard. You can guess how that ended.

I had a similar situation one winter while sledding. There's a perfect hill in our neighborhood—the powder was deep and fresh and that particular day we were using large innertubes as our sleds. Those who know this activity know the worst part of sledding is the hike back up the hill after your run. Kelly, my ingenious husband, had made the process much easier by pulling us back up to the top with a snowmobile. After our descent we used a rope to attach the inner tube, then we hopped on the back of the snowmobile. My husband would cart us back up to the top with the tube trailing behind. After several runs, the rope we were using for transport detached and was buried somewhere in the snow. With his innovative mind in peak shape, Kelly decided that was no big deal. At the bottom of the hill, he instructed me to loop one arm through the hole of the innertube and latch on to him with the other arm as he pulled me behind him on the snowmobile. It would save time anyway. I was understandably skeptical. Our success relied on too many external factors I had no control over, and the ones I did have control over (my strength and coordination) were going to be put to a test I lacked faith in. While it seemed like a bad idea, the only other option I could see was the hike.

At the expense of being called, "chicken," I reluctantly hopped on behind him, hooked my arm around the tube and gritted my teeth. I stayed aboard for maybe two seconds. The awkward weight of the tube when he punched the throttle yanked me back, and I ended up face down in the snow.

What's important to note is that in both these situations, I knew better! Both times I remember being hesitant and even putting up a protest. But both times I let someone else control me when I should have and *could* have controlled myself.

Think of the last time you were frustrated. Frustration is a control issue, it happens for one of two reasons—you want to control something you can't, or you are letting something control you that you shouldn't (like the past or the future). From the Taoist principle of "stillness" we learn:

> *"Grief and disappointment come from outside yourself.*
> *Lock your door on them. Be rid of them... you will find*
> *that the greatest joy of all is just to be."*[38]

Emotions that follow triggers, such as frustration or anger, are by this very definition, reactive. Once you can identify the trigger, or the primary stressor that baits your anger, you'll begin to gain more control, becoming the master of your responses rather than their servant. On the topic of anger—when someone gets angry, whose problem is it? Theirs. When someone gets angry at *you*, whose problem is that? Still theirs. Don't let it become yours.

Ever find yourself saying things like, "That makes me so happy." "That makes me so sad." You're giving your control away. Now don't feel too bad about it. We're built with chemicals designed to respond. Those responses are indicators that everything is working as it should. But deep within yourself is the ability to take the reins of those emotions when they do come. You get better and better and quicker and quicker until you get to the point where you can intercept those chemicals between stimulus and response.

Exceptions:
- There are abusive situations that are totally out of our control. I am so sorry for those who find themselves there. When those situations are observed, you must find what you *can* control and hold on to it. However, "toxic" situations are not out of your control. Once you recognize the difference between abuse and toxicity, you're empowered to act rather than react.

- Sometimes it's important to let someone lead. Situations that fall into this category—when you really don't have the ability to make a decision, if your mental health is unstable, if you're overwhelmed or in a bad state. These may require that you give control to someone who you know has your best interest until you can regain the reins. (How vital is your team-selection in these cases?)

SHELF

During an especially difficult time, I was with my dad at a major event with lots of publicity. He, knowing me as perhaps only a parent can, said something I'll never forget. *"You're like a duck on the water, Heather. Cool and calm for everyone to see but struggling like hell underneath."* There are some things (and some times) we simply cannot control. But that doesn't mean we can't compartmentalize. Every part of me that day wanted to throw a temper tantrum. But I found my composure and reigned it in, knowing I would attend to my inner storm at another time.

Another control trick I find really helpful is to have an imaginary shelf to put issues on when I can't attend to them at the moment. Our ability to function during times of grief, frustration, or other potentially debilitating emotions will depend on it. No matter how good you are at juggling, life's unpredictability will always be throwing more balls at you. To stay in business, you need a system for superfluous balls.

Your figurative shelf should be small and simple, with room enough for only a couple of things. It's easily accessible but out of the way. When something comes up that you're not ready for, decide which issue to deal with at present and which to set on the shelf for later. It helps avoid the immobilization that can come from getting overwhelmed. (A balm for those of us who struggle with multi-tasking.)

Situations will arise that will try to knock you out. I'm neither advocating nor condoning the dismissal of strong emotions every time they arise. *You control you* by deciding which items to put on the shelf. Sometimes, the emotion is the thing to be attended to first. The shelf is not intended to aid denial. It's intended to open up space for clarity. When "passion bubbles are very near the surface"[39] it's not a great time for decision making. When you feel that temperature rising, resist the urge to react. Gain control by putting the issue on hold, promising to confront it later.

Shelves have two principal benefits:
- Since you're postponing and not dismissing, it allows you to take some weight off your shoulders and give yourself totally to the present moment without distraction, knowing there will be a future time to deal with it. Some situations can be debilitating and you can't just check out of life when trouble comes. You still need to function, work, socialize, learn, teach, eat. The shelf is designed to give you respite when you need it. Good therapists aren't always on call. They schedule appointments.
- Things tend to cool down on the shelf. As emotions rise, objectivity tends to decline. In the heat of the moment you can lose your senses and ultimately your composure. There are times and situations when you just ain't got time for that! In those moments, it's okay to say to yourself, "I'm gonna worry, cry, scream, rage about this... later." Then, when you make time later, you approach the shelf with intention. Don't be surprised if the awaiting item is less intimidating than before.

Time is an excellent mitigator. The intensity of emotions diminishes when you don't give them your energy, and in the interim, a well-kept shelf has some clarifying properties. Sometimes you'll see clearly as soon as you pick a shelved decision up, that it's right... or wrong. Sometimes you'll have to do a little more considering, but your perspective of the thing will likely not be the same as it was when you first placed it on the shelf. Shelves are magic like that.

Examples of things to put on the shelf:
- a tough decision
- a stressful obligation
- worrisome news that's relevant but not imminent
- a grief you haven't addressed
- personal mistakes or failures
- large purchases

Not kidding about that last one. Any time I'm about to make a significant purchase, it goes on the shelf. In fact, I have a mandatory 24-hour rule if an acquisition will potentially strain my budget. Salesmen dislike my rule, but it gets me out of those sticky high-pressure moments when they're trying to seal the deal. *"I love it. I love you! I definitely want to make this purchase right now, but you see... I have this rule."* Magic, indeed.

Now the warning... Just forgetting about a troubling issue for a period does us no good. Give it time to breathe and get busy with other things, but there's a reason we're talking about a shelf not a closet or a garbage disposal. It's a small space and doesn't have room for clutter so respect it for what it is—a tool of self-compassion. Putting something on the shelf is honoring that thing—as long as you make time to revisit it within a reasonable time period. Pick it back up. Neglect is an ugly word in every way it's used.

In summary, when you get in a stressful situation, there are

87

two productive actions you can take—help the situation or help yourself deal with it. To succeed with either, you must allow yourself to focus only on what you can control. Don't cast blame or throw shame. And unless you're a sky marshal, don't try to control another person. It'll backfire anyway. Then get out of the worry weeds. One helpful activity is this—write down everything that's stressing you out. Then go back through your list, cross out whatever you can't control and circle the ones you can. Zero in on those and get busy, focusing on the present, recognizing what you can control, and acting intentionally.

DISCOMFORT

✓ Starters are comfortable with being uncomfortable

I've come to realize a big reason why I love Rocky so much. It's not because he's a fighter. Not because he's a winner, not because he's a scruffy kid from the slums that makes it big. It's because he can take a beating.

When you've made a decision and you feel good about it, or have taken an action toward your goal, don't be surprised when opposition shows up. It will *always* show up when you're on the right track. Don't take it as a sign that you made the wrong choice. See it as a test. Its purpose is to see if you've got what it takes. If you want to get to the endzone, there's going to be lineman in your path. So don't let discomfort interrupt you.

People with strong personalities, or those who know themselves a little too confidently, tend to paint themselves into a corner. But what if the world needs something different from you? What if you're meant to change? The benefits of stretching outweigh the benefits of stoicism, even when you're in a good place. "You" should be a fluid term, always remember that. Never betray your core values and principles but push your limits when you feel it may be right. Just because it's uncomfortable doesn't mean it's not for you.

There is too much evidence to ignore that discomfort is vital medicine:

- Do you improve your health without changing your diet/exercise regime?
- Can you build strength without tearing your muscles?
- Have you ever met an all-star athlete who didn't put in extra hours of practice?
- Can you make more money (legally) without taking up extra hours at work?
- Can you make new friends if you remain in your same comfortable circle?

If you were taught to pray as a child, how were you taught to pray? On your knees? If you practice meditation, do you use hero pose or crossed legs? You were probably taught these poses are important because they facilitate energy or signal humility. True. But here's why an otherwise unnatural position works—because it's uncomfortable. It keeps you focused. Ever try to pray lying in bed? It just doesn't work. When we're comfortable, we're more easily distracted. Minds wander, attention fades, comfort reigns.

Another Stanford University psychiatrist, Dr. Anna Lembke, specializes in addiction. She has witnessed profound conclusions about discomfort. "We're all running from pain. Some of us take pills. Some of us couch surf while binge-watching Netflix. Some of us read romance novels. We'll do almost anything to distract ourselves from ourselves. Yet all this trying to insulate ourselves from pain seems only to have made our pain worse."[40]

Consider this. If you think back to a time you were most fulfilled, did you get there by being comfortable?

There's no way to get what you want without doing something you probably don't wanna do. People who have reached their

89

lofty goals have gotten comfortable with being uncomfortable. They have aligned their aspirations with actions. So make sure you're regularly finding discomfort in all areas of your life: physical, mental, spiritual, and social. It's the best way to grow.

———— • ————

Several years ago, my neighbor was thinning her irises and decided that rather than disposing of the superfluous bulbs, she'd toss them out on an ugly, unkempt, rocky part of the yard. Considering them dispensable, she had no intention of upkeep. She would just see if they naturally took root.

They did survive, but they didn't blossom. Each Spring, green shoots would sprout up just as their relatives across the yard, but they didn't bloom. Too bad, she thought, but oh well. They would turn yellow and wane as the summer passed, never producing the big flowers the other irises did. After a few Springs, her husband planted a tree near the neglected irises. He loved that tree and gave a lot of attention to it, consistently and thoroughly watering the new tree. The water did what it tends to do, it seeped over to the irises in the nearby abandoned rock bed. That summer we saw those discarded bulbs as we never had before. Their big beautiful purple petals taught me that extra nurture can reveal a hidden nature.

There was nothing wrong with the irises internally. They were successfully going through their perennial life cycle. But why simply exist when you can bloom?

Even when you understand that struggle is a necessary part of growth, how often do you seek it out? Should you? Or should you simply accept your weaknesses and take on only the struggles that naturally come your way? When looking at load management, I suggest you embrace discomfort a little more readily. See what you can add, embrace, incorporate into your routine to ensure you stay building. Because when you're comfortable, you're not growing.

The DNA of the iris didn't change when it was watered. It always had the potential, it just needed to be fed. Discomfort is the food you need for development. With ease there is no progress. With struggle, comes opportunity. That struggle to turn a weakness into a strength may be exactly what you need.

Brené Brown calls self-compassion the *core of mental toughness*. So ask yourself which is more compassionate, watering your weaknesses or leaving them in the rock bed as they are? I propose that we can have compassion for ourselves without being complacent about our weaknesses. In reality, the most compassionate thing we can do for ourselves is turn our weaknesses over to God and work together on turning them into strengths. Now keep in mind some weaknesses just take time. And sometimes, time is not on our side. Putting the errant parts of ourselves on the shelf temporarily can be liberating as long as we look forward with patience and hope, returning at some point to those shortcomings with faith. Believe in grace as did Jeremiah, "Be not afraid for I am with thee to deliver thee."[41]

All the world shares one common direction and every organic thing on this earth is in a process—growing or decaying. Each living thing teaches us that growth is in the struggle. Make sure you're moving in a positive direction by using every experience as a life lesson. The world only spins one direction.

Blooming requires discomfort. You've got to be willing to break out of that comfort zone and do what you were meant to do. Even in the tough times, reach. Grow. After all, it's the darkest clouds that have been watering your flowers all along.

GOALS
For some people, goals are an impetus, but for others, goals can be another impediment. Whether it's fear, discouragement, or the prospect of not achieving the goals, the possibility of unmet expectations is just too risky. No one likes to fail. For those who

hesitate to set goals, there's a simple mindset shift that can make a huge difference.

Of all the data on achievement, this one's my favorite:
100% of the people who don't set goals, don't achieve them.

Don't fail before you've even started. One constructive aspect of action is that, like the shelf, it clarifies the goal or the decision. If you're standing in the dark, looking down two pathways with only a flashlight, your vision only goes so far. You must take a few steps to confirm it's the path you want. And with each step, that vision becomes clearer. When you find yourself not measuring up, consider you may be measuring the wrong thing. Dan Sullivan makes a strong case for measuring backwards in his book, *The Gap and the Gain: The High Achievers' Guide to Happiness, Confidence and Success.*

"The way to measure your progress is backward against where you started, not against your ideal."
Dan Sullivan

According to his research, people who overfocus on the distance they must go to reach a goal accomplish much less (and are much less fulfilled) than those who, instead, consider how far they've come. The objective needs not be the goal specifically, but the movement toward it. When you fall short, don't waste time lamenting your lack. Praise yourself for the distance you gained. Let progress be the new goal.

If you were hoping for an outline of how to set and achieve goals, sorry to disappoint you—but not really. It's wise to be skeptical of prescribed processes, especially when it comes to something as personal as goals. Don't get online and glean from celebrities who are disconnected from your personal circumstances, as if they only proclaim the honest truth. Don't swallow prescriptions from people who don't know you. There are a gazillion strategies for meeting goals and increasing productivity. Gather them like blocks then build your own personalized strategy by consulting your identity, your higher power, or a member of your team. Ultimately consult yourself and build something custom fit, taking advice because it's right for *you*.

I remember printing out a 5-minute productivity plan from a well-known coach. As it was inching out of the printer, I had this lightbulb moment... she doesn't know me. She doesn't know my strengths or my weaknesses. I've been incredibly productive for almost half a century. In fact, I coach *others* on improving their productivity. Why am I letting someone else tell me how to do something I'm an expert at? It was set up nicely and organized, and I liked the way it looked. Great! So I took that and built my own.

There are so many blocks to help you build. Gather ideas looking at different productivity plans, goal setting tips, etc. Leading entity in the goal setting and achieving industry, Franklin Covey, expounds on four disciplines of execution: set, act, track, and report.[42] The number of goal-setting resources is immeasurable, but they all depend on one common factor—how well you control you. Figure out what's important to you and what works for your life, learning about what drives your personal sustainable movement. Above all, act. Keep these goal-setting principles in mind:

- A goal isn't a life sentence. Many people are hesitant to set goals because they're worried about not achieving them. If you dislike goals because you don't like the pressure or commitment, remember it's the *progress* that matters. Don't let yourself be disappointed when you don't meet a goal—as long as you make progress, that's what matters.
- When aiming at a physical target your focus must bridge the gap between the distant goal and

the immediate action. This level of discipline can be difficult—it's easy to be so consumed with a distant goal you forget to take a step. On the contrary, if you get carried away by the task at hand and forget to look up, you will miss the mark. When you set a goal, keep it in your vision, but the trick is to not let it be your sole focus. The grind is at the step in front of you. Look up frequently to make sure your trajectory is still in line but keep your feet on the ground.

You've been warned about establishing expectations outside of your control. While each small step you take has only a minimal contribution to your end goal, it can monumentally influence your trajectory. So make sure it's controlled. Too many outside factors are at play and there is an overabundance of difficult circumstances in the world. Tragedy can be found in every corner. It compels us to want to either act or react. Choose action.

An exercise I like to use with clients is to ask them to score themselves on the possibility of reaching a goal. Honestly assess how likely you are to follow through. Then ask if there is anything that would improve those odds. Be a fan of goals but not so much with expectations.

One horrific event close to my home was the abduction of Elizabeth Smart. I struggle to understand how humanity can allow such sorrow and abuse, but then I see the incredible outreach and service that The Elizabeth Smart Foundation achieves...all because of her misfortune. Do the benefits from this organization justify the abuse? No, we can't say that it does. But the example it gives of proactivity is an ensign for action. It helps to right a wrong, allowing a world of positive to blossom from a negative act. It's beauty for ashes.[43]

I'M NOT THE VICTIM. I'M THE BOSS.

SUMMARY

"May your past be the sound of your feet upon the ground."
Nate Ruess

It's normal to want clarity before taking a big step. But answers don't come without action. And the quicker you move along a path, the sooner you'll know if it's the right one or the wrong one. Courage and a "cause" are needed to get started. Control will help you maintain it.

Time for the warning: It's easy to get caught up in your new level of production. Reaching milestones, making positive changes and seeing results, completing new tasks, these all have the potential to give you a really nice dopamine hit. It feels amazing and therefore operates like a drug. But too much of anything, even a good thing, can threaten to overwhelm and even control you. It can throw off that ever-important balance. Keep your productivity in check. Tips in the final chapter.

Be assured that each action item in this book is 100% within your control. Let go of what you can't control and seize what you can. Embrace discomfort as a necessary part of growth. Question your goals and the process you're taking to reach them.

Step is another word with both a noun and verb variation. Again, use the verb—it's more productive. How many gym memberships go underutilized? It's not the membership that makes a difference in your health or performance. It's not the transaction, the routine or the commitment. It's the amount of movement that makes the difference.

The best predictor of the future is the past. Want to know what the next year holds in store for you? Take a look at the past six to twelve months of your life—that's your trend. Start closing the gap between where you are and where you're going with intentional action.

There are no obstacles too big *for starters*.

Starters Aim to Give

"The meaning of life is to find your gift. The purpose of life is to give it away."
Pablo Picasso

Giving is not just a moral obligation or selfless act; it is a cornerstone of personal development and fulfillment. The act of giving—whether of time, talents, resources, or energy—is essential to achieving our highest potential and connecting with the world around us. Scientific studies, life lessons, and even nature itself demonstrate that giving is the catalyst for true progress.

This next step may be the most controversial, but it's worth consideration. Stay with me and remember the value of discomfort because here's a hard truth to swallow—it's not always about you. Your purpose extends beyond yourself. While we've discussed the importance of identity, let's clarify: you are a vessel, a vital instrument, but an instrument nonetheless. Your identity, your talents, and your efforts are the means, not the end. The end is to give.

For starters, giving is easy. If you aren't a giver, you'll be like the irises that refused to bloom. You'll be existing only, but for what purpose? You cannot grow until you give. Giving is a specific and necessary type of discomfort if you want to achieve your potential.

Here's a different angle. You've probably noticed some people are innately givers, and others takers. You may be thinking right now of specific individuals in your circle who fit each label. I have a handful of friends that only take. They don't inspire me or sustain me. So why am I still calling them friends? My best answer to that question is another question. Is the only objective of existence our own personal development and improvement?

Trending ideas suggest you shouldn't be friends with people who don't help you grow—you don't owe loyalty to anyone who isn't a positive influence in your life. These suggestions are well-founded as they support the theory that your team must be aligned with your identity. Amen to that. But is there value to having people in your life who, though they don't help you grow, help you give?

College students at the University of British Columbia participated in an experiment headed by social psychologist Liz Dunn, where they were given an envelope containing some cash. Half the group had to spend the money (various amounts ranging between $5-$20) by 5pm on themselves. The other half of the group had to spend the money on someone else by 5pm. Prior to the study, the students were given a happiness assessment and then hypothesized that those who got to spend money on themselves would be happier at the end of the experiment. But the assessment proved the contrary—the happiness scale tipped the other way.[44] (Measured by self-reported data, behavioral observations, and physiological indicators). The givers were happier than the takers.

The truth is, we are meant to give, it's how we're wired. If we're not giving, we're not reaching our potential. Again, all living things teach us there can actually be no growth without giving. Giving makes a positive ripple, it increases positive energy for both the giver and receiver. To always seek our own interest above others is to waste energy we could be spending bettering the world around us.

Selfishness
is the absence
of love.

"Think about the times in your life when you have felt
most alive and engaged. Who and what were you
focused on in those moments—on yourself or
on something bigger that included others?"
The Outward Mindset, The Arbinger Institute

So much pain and discomfort comes from focusing on self. Turn that focus outward and you'll see your problems fade into the background. Knowing I'm a professional and certified coach, people frequently call me up for free coaching. They don't call it that, they just say hello and start spilling their guts. It's an unspoken friends and family discount code I guess, but I honestly couldn't be happier about it. If I have a skill or a gift that can help someone when they really truly need it, I want to feel free about giving. It's my way of maintaining control. Everyone has something to share and we should be more content to do so.

Look around at all you have. In 2021, the World Health Organization (WHO) and the United Nations Children's Fund (UNICEF) estimated that 2 billion people worldwide lack access to clean water.[45] Around 40% of Americans aren't making ends meet. Roughly one billion people across the globe don't even have shoes. Consider all you've been given. How can you share and bless those around you?

But I have nothing to give! I've heard it before and will hear it again. And I couldn't disagree more. Here's a thought—you have you. Giving is as simple as one, two, three. Here are three gifts you need to make sure you are giving regularly if you want to reach your potential and really thrive. They are all possible. For everyone. Yes you.

ONE

Give your gift.

And give it freely. You never know who it might affect. Monetization of your gifts was mentioned in the section on Identity. Many people have made great livings selling their hobbies, and that's wonderful, but just be warned that as soon as a hobby, talent, or gift is used to make money, it becomes a job. Being a source of income gives it the potential to *control* you. Be aware that attaching a price tag can potentially devalue the benefits for both you and your recipients. Remember, with regard to those creative hobbies, personal fulfillment doesn't come from the capital. It comes from the creating.

Warnings: How much is too much to give? It is possible to give too much. In simple terms, there are two ways to know when you've given too much: If you begin to lose your identity or if you enable the other party, you've gone too far.

Everyone has their own line between giving and being taken advantage of, and you must identify yours. If you control you, then you'll learn how to set those boundaries. Boundaries are not selfish or unkind, so don't let anyone convince you otherwise. They are a sign of love and respect for both parties. Draw them clearly and enjoy the protection they offer. If you need help defining a boundary, start by distinguishing when something isn't your problem. This will help keep the takers from taking too much.

Shortly after I stopped selling my art, I received a message from an acquaintance. It was long, so I've trimmed her statement for clarity but have not otherwise altered her message:

"I wanted to thank you for being inspired to paint such a beautiful picture. Earlier this year I was struggling... I was scrolling through Facebook one day and came across your page for your art. When I saw that painting I had so many different thoughts and feelings hit me at once... I just wanted to let you know because that painting has changed my life. Thank you."

A couple things to note: First, she completely misinterpreted the painting. What she saw wasn't what I intended for her to see. Second, it is extremely difficult for me to post images of myself or my work online. Quality therapy sessions are required for me to be active on social media and this post was no exception. So for my gift to have such a profound effect, do you think there was a higher power at play? A power that influenced my hands, heart, and eyes... and hers?

The unexpected impact of giving without seeking recognition taught me where to place value. When we dial into our gifts and use them as they were intended, the universe bends, and the positive gains exceed the giver's investment. How can someone gain more than we give? Like the ripples from a single drop, it's magic.

TWO

Give to your team.

Giving doesn't have to be physical or tangible, the most impactful gifts aren't. It doesn't need to involve money or even much time or energy. The only requirement by definition is its free transfer from you to anywhere/anyone else.

You may have been thinking, when considering your coaches, teammates, and fans, *Sorry, Hj, there is a VERY important individual in my life that is actually none of these roles.* To this I respond, Ah, but who are you to them? (Parents and guardians, listen up. You have the ability to be all three of these roles for your child.)

When you identify someone in your life who fits none of the

qualifications to be an influencer on your team, you have a choice. You can cut them out. No harm in that, in fact it's what a lot of coaches and therapists will tell you to do—drop the dead weight. But here's where true leaders can emerge. Assuming there's no abuse or harm to you in doing so, figure out what you can give. Can you be a coach, teammate or fan to them?

———————— • • ————————

As I sat to eat my breakfast, I kept my phone close, anticipating a text from my daughter who would be arriving at school right then and heading to the gym doors to check the taped-up lists for her name.

Finally, the phone rang. She didn't make the ballroom dance team.

This girl. She has a 4.0 grade point average. She's a starter on the basketball team, has already secured a spot on the Robotics team, and is hopeful to make the volleyball team as well. I really needed her to *not* make the ballroom team.

So the first emotion I felt when reading her text was relief. But immediately, that emotion shifted to sympathy. My little girl was disappointed. Poor thing. She really wanted this.

So I started texting and my instincts (they're not always right) were to tell her what a blessing that was because now she could focus on her other activities and not be overwhelmed. Again, I caught myself. At that moment, she didn't need a coach. She needed a fan. That difference matters.

Right then, she needed more than to be seen, she needed to belong.

Remembering how important your team is to your success, ask yourself what role you are filling in someone else's team. Are you a coach or a mentor? Could you be a better teammate to someone who is in real need of your strength? Who can you advocate for? One major aspect of your identity is how you show up to others. You're not fully maximized until you're being each one of these roles in the life of someone else. You've had plenty of experiences. So from what you've been given, find where you have the privilege of influence and give. Review the Team section and ask where you could be making a difference in the life of someone else. How can you be better at each particular role?

When someone trusts you to occupy a space in their life, be aware of their needs. If a person you value is vulnerable with you, it's critical you know what role they are seeking you to fill. As you consider giving to your team, keep these in mind:

Coach: Your opportunities to be a coach will be rare, so cherish them. It's a privilege, not a right, to be a coach. Two things you need are permission and credibility. You are an expert at something. You can mentor someone, but you need to be invited to that role. When you receive that invitation, stay humble. It's not about you. We all know someone who sees and attacks our every flaw, right? Givers of unsolicited advice are jerks. Coaching is a lot less about telling people what to do and a lot more about understanding. People want to be in control. Most will follow through with their own ideas better than yours.

Maya Angelou penned, *"Few, if any, survive their teens. Most surrender to the vague but murderous pressure of adult conformity."* When coaching young people, see and accept them where they are. Don't judge or assume, give them the space and confidence they need to feel safe. A good coach knows those boundaries because they know their subject.

To accept them does not mean to enable them. Your influence will never trump agency. When you put the ball in someone else's court, let it go and prepare for the return.

When someone comes to you in distress, natural coaches instinctively jump into the coaching role, but that may not be what they need. When they fall, it's not your job to pick them up. It's your job to teach them to pick themselves up. On the rare occasion a rescue is in order... go big. Leave them no doubt of your support.

Then keep your mouth shut. This is not the time for lectures. Let them be grateful.

Some ways to quickly discredit yourself:
- Tell them you know what they're going through.
- Be distracted.
- Be insincere or dishonest (try too hard).

Is it possible to over-coach? Definitely. You'll know you've gone too far when they stop listening, so remember that no one ever made a difference by talking a lot. Be sensitive to that line and don't cross it. Too often leaders of an older generation will project, expecting their progeny to behave based on the leaders' experiences. If you've been on the planet during a different time and culture, not only are your experiences different, the world is a different place. Mind the generational gap.

Leaders tend to get preachy. It's the nature of the position—they talk too much. But great leaders understand the value of communication and fully endorse what Thomas Erikson said about it happening "on the listener's terms." If you were to look at a transcript of the most effective coaching sessions, you'd find the conversations were dominated by the client. The best leaders, coaches, parents, teachers are exceptional listeners. And they listen not with the intent to respond, but with the intent to understand and empathize. Bill Nye said, *"Everyone you will ever meet knows something you don't."* So resist the urge to be a puppeteer. Let them lead.

Teammate: Your opportunities to be a teammate will be sporadic and varied. Just as you need an invitation to be a coach, you need connection to be a teammate, so identify and eliminate whatever bars you from that connection.

Rocky taught Paulie why Adrian was about to be his best teammate, "She got gaps. I got gaps. Together we fill the gaps."

Again, mind that gap. Use your best communication skills to build a bridge, then strengthen your team by offering your best self. Know that fitting in isn't the same as belonging. Stay unique and true to your identity. It's a privilege to be part of a team, no matter the position or role you have on that team. Shift that mindset and be a giver.

How to discredit yourself as a teammate:
- Coach.
- Compare.

Don't critique or counsel without invitation—that's not your role here. When they want your advice, they'll ask for it. Don't make unnecessary observations. Comparison should only happen between self and self. What they need is your presence, your strength, your lack of judgement and your solidarity.

Thomas Reid's "Essays on the Intellectual Powers of Man," published in 1786, popularized the idiom "a chain is no stronger than its weakest link." This theory may be considered fact in the context of physics, but when it comes to people and teams, it is philosophical BS.

Athletes know that when a muscle is strained, other muscles take over and compensate. Material scientists know that weaker fibers may still work effectively within the structure because stronger materials around them absorb and redistribute stress, leading to a stronger overall structure. Leaders know that if a load can be redistributed across multiple points rather than concentrating stress on the weakest part, the system can perform beyond what the weak link alone would support.

I believe the weakest link has value and can indeed strengthen the whole. Remember, when something isn't measuring up, you may be measuring the wrong thing.

Fan: Your opportunities to be a fan are endless and there are no prerequisites. Anyone can be a fan to anyone at any time, so what holds us back?

Is it the absence of personal benefit? Shouldn't be. The best way to get a fan is to be one.

Is it the investment or buy in? Shouldn't be. It's minimal.

Is it the idea that lifting someone else brings us down? Shouldn't be. Because that's bull.

Is it perception? Well, that's pride talking and you've been warned about pride. You will be judged by who you choose to support, there's no avoiding it, so be prepared to defend that choice and ask yourself what matters most.

✓ Starters are the best benchwarmers

Just try it. If you really want to be a starter, try out that bench seat, see what difference you can make from the back row. For no reason and for nothing to gain, find someone to hype. Be an advocate. And be loud about it.

How to discredit yourself as a fan:
- Hold out for fair weather.
- Be easily distracted.

If you walk away when the going gets rough, you've failed the only test that matters. Stay when your subject is down. Give patience and understanding when they are angry. Give acceptance when they fall short and respect when they fail. Your job is to love them at their worst.

In all these roles, don't over-promise and under-deliver. People aren't stupid. You may sell them on something once, but you'll never earn loyalty or trust or repeat business if you underdeliver. Give a little something extra to surprise them. Being close to you should have added perks, so consult your identity about what

112

special thing you can give for those who allow you to take space in their lives.

I believe the best team we'll ever have can and should be in our own homes. That is not the reality for many people, but it is still the ideal. If you find yourself a victim of a poor Team Fam, what can you do to make a better one? If you are blessed with these critical roles within the walls of your own home, are you giving back? Chances are you fill multiple roles, so be aware of who they need you to be with every interaction. Do they need your opinion or your confidence? Your counsel, approval, or silence?

Among a myriad of reasons the family has been dubbed the basic and most important unit of society, here are my two favorites:

- Accountability. Goodness knows these people keep us in check and humble.
- Opportunity to forgive and to ask forgiveness.

THREE

Forgive.

In life, incredible light comes from forgiveness. But light cannot be recognized without darkness. A certain dark presence wants to convince us that forgiveness equates with loss—that when we forgive, we're letting go of something valuable, that we lose control if we let go of resentment. Let this be the lesson of the day: Don't take lessons from darkness.

━━━━● ● ●━━━

Kelly was in trouble, and I initiated the silent treatment. He knew he was in trouble but didn't know why, and I wasn't going to tell him if he didn't care to find out. Have you ever been in a similar situation? I let my frustrations fester and build. At first, it took me some time to calm down. When I did, though, I realized his behavior, though wrong and hurtful, was a result of some major stress and frustration he was dealing with. That was no excuse, but I realized if I couldn't stand by him at his worst, I wasn't the wife he deserved.

But there was still the problem of penitence. He wasn't apologizing. Wasn't even seeking to know what he'd done wrong. How could he be so callous? That's when I realized my forgiveness wasn't for him. It was for me. So after a while (too long), I told him I was ready to not be mad anymore. Everything went back to normal.

The offense was his, but the problem was mine. First, I should've communicated to him immediately what he'd done that was so offensive. Second, I shouldn't have fed my frustrations, exacerbating the issue.

In the Bible, there are six different words (three Hebrew and three Greek) that were all translated into the same English word—"forgive." Much was lost in translation. It's important to recognize that *forgive* has many meanings. We do not have the right, nor the ability to remove guilt and consequences. My favorite is the Hebrew "nasa" which connotes lifting up. When we *nasa* someone, we lift the burden not only from them but from ourselves. While there is only One who can wholly forgive, we are required to forgive everyone, always.

Even if they're not sorry, especially if they're not aware.

"Thee lift me, and I'll lift thee,
and we will ascend together."
Quaker Proverb

Forgiveness is the pinnacle of control—an ultimate hallmark of one who has mastered themselves. All you lose are chains, negativity, anxiety, and darkness, making more room for light. True forgiveness does not equal enabling, it does not excuse bad behavior, what it does is liberate you from emotional bondage. True forgiveness is not always possible on your own, you may need to employ a team. It's not just worth it, it's necessary.

FORGIVENESS IS THE FINAL STEP OF SEPARATING YOURSELF FROM SOMEONE ELSE'S BAD BEHAVIOR.

Therefore...

All the more reason to... forgive yourself.

My dearest friend had to give a presentation to a religious group. Her theme was "Heavenly Help" and after a powerful speech she planned to conclude her message by playing the song "[I Believe There Are] Angels Among As" by Alabama. This was in the early 1990s so '80s country was still in its heyday. At the time, two-song albums were still around, and she had the single on a cd that she put in the cd player, all cued up and ready for the big finale. At the end of her remarks, she hit play and took a moment to relax, basking in the culmination of all her preparation. She soaked in her daze for a full minute before she was pulled back into reality by a sense of something unfamiliar. She identified it immediately. The cd player was on track two, not track one, and Alabama was well into their chorus of "Give It All You've Got". At this point she had two choices. She could stop the song, apologize, and restart. Or she could embrace the shift. The mood was gone so she rolled with it. At the end of the song, she was compelled to make a final statement, so she said, "Let's go out there and *give it all we've got!*"

Maybe you have to know her and her trademark elegance and poise to appreciate this story, but what I love most about this blunder is that she just kept on. She forgave herself immediately, knowing there was nothing she could do to remediate. She forged ahead, letting go of a mistake she could have let haunt her.

SUMMARY

Remember that to give by definition is to freely transfer.
Let. It. Go.

Don't give selfishly and don't give grudgingly. Change your status from *given* to *giving*.

Identity and offering may seem counterintuitive. But giving becomes a burden only when it's something you weren't meant to give. Recall that the objective of realizing your true identity is to maximize your contribution to the whole. If you're solid on your identity, and acting in alignment with it, giving of yourself becomes a gain, not a loss, to your true self. So rather than opposites, they are like yin and yang, existing in harmony, dually dependent on one another.

Despair, discouragement, and depression are real. Being overwhelmed happens. During these dark clouded times, it may seem you cannot give. That is the darkness talking, and we know better now, don't we?

> *"Our deepest fear is not that we are inadequate. Our deepest fear is that we are powerful beyond measure. It is our light, not our darkness that most frightens us. We ask ourselves, 'Who am I to be brilliant, gorgeous, talented, fabulous?' Actually, who are you not to be? You are a child of God. Your playing small does not serve the world. There is nothing enlightened about shrinking so that other people won't feel insecure around you. We are all meant to shine, as children do. We were born to make manifest the glory of God that is within us. It's not just in some of us, it's in everyone. And as we let our own light shine, we unconsciously give other people permission to do the same. As we are liberated from our own fear, our presence automatically liberates others."*
> Marianne Williamson

116

I mentioned in the beginning that these steps were to be considered arbitrary, but let's call them cyclical. When you feel like you've mastered them all, end where you began... with gratitude. It's one of the easiest things you can give.

When you are self-conscious, insecure, or feeling out of place, release those binding chains by turning your focus outward. When it seems like the world is closing in on you, give. When you're overwhelmed, give. When you feel terribly alone, give. When you feel like you have nothing left to give, find a way to give.

Giving is natural *for starters.*

Finishing Is a Matter of Clarity

*"The key to success is to start before you're
ready and finish before you're done."*

Richie Norton*attributed

A book for starters would be incomplete if it didn't at least graze the topic of finishing, would it not? But figuratively, finish lines are much more difficult to define than starting lines. The truth is, not all starters finish by the same standards. Which begs the question, what does it mean to finish anyway? What are those standards and who writes them? It's a hazy concept.

Finishing isn't about clinging to goals at all costs. It's about matching your actions with your identity, courageously persevering when it's right, and humbly pivoting when it's not.

Every great coach will tell you they have their starters and they also have their finishers. When it matters most, when the game is on the line, it's the finishers they rely on.

When we began, the objective was to maximize productivity. Now we'll look at *optimizing* impact. You've come a long way, whether you realize it or not. And true starters know how to finish—not by crossing a line or hitting a target, but by having a deeper understanding of what it means to finish strong. So let's attempt to draw some finish lines.

LINES

To finish is to have the guts to continue when the steps disappear. Some finish lines are clear, with a course laid out in perfect, established steps to achievement. Other finish lines are similarly clear, but with a more ambiguous path leading to them. There are many ways to reach the same destination.

What do the following movies have in common?
- Remember the Titans (2000)
- La La Land (2016)
- The Karate Kid (1984)
- Dead Poets Society (1989)
- Rocky, of course

These stories show how letting go of established practices can pave the way for innovation and groundbreaking success.

This is not to say that prescribed paths can't be useful. Choosing a pre-established course with the finish line you desire is nothing to be ashamed of... as long as you choose it. Courses and finish lines are drawn by many people, but the only ones that matter are the ones you select for yourself. You control you (last time, I promise).

Whether you choose your own course or follow the one laid out for you, persist.

✓ Starters make no excuses

Do you find yourself saying, "I'll get this done today, as long as..." How about, "If nothing else comes up, I'm going to..." Drop the ifs.

What do the following people have in common?
- Edward Shackleton
- Malala Yousafzai
- Elon Musk
- Steven Hawking

Despite all odds, they persevered. Research any of their histories to be inspired by endurance.

Finishing is an art.

At age 22, I met someone who was as much a starter as I was, so I married him. He came from a very different background and hadn't had a lesson in anything other than sports, but he

124

was a starter through and through. Together we've started five businesses. Some of them didn't work out, a few of them really have. Remember, a starter uses what's available to make a change. Rich or poor, you can take advantage of every opportunity.

To finish also means to have the guts *not* to step, even when it's laid out in front of you. Making personal changes, especially when they deal with your identity, takes immense courage. Courage to say, "I've changed my mind" or even "I've made a mistake," which means you want to learn. It opens the door to improvement and perspective.

It bears repeating. Courage and balance are so much better than confidence.

With all your ventures, you'll hit a point with each one where you have to push through discomfort. It's at that point you'll have to decide if your identity is in line and your goal is worth it. If the two aren't fully in sync, quit. Does that mean you're not a finisher? Not in the least. It allows you to move on to more starting.

> *"The beautiful thing about learning is no*
> *one can take it away from you."*
> *Blues icon, B.B. King*

DEAD ENDS

Closed doors, like wrong roads, have tremendous value. Don't worry too much about paths that don't take you as far as you hoped. There is wisdom and growth in experience, no matter how it ends. Eliminating an option is as valuable as choosing one.

As a grade schooler, I really got into gymnastics. Side note— I'm 5'10" and had all the indicators of reaching that height from a young age. I had done a school report on Mary-Lou Retton and her coach, Béla Károlyi, after Mary-Lou had just won five medals (and my heart) at the 1984 Summer Olympics. She was iconic! And I was ready to be her. I asked my parents to let me take gymnastics lessons, so they found a gym and a great coach, some cute sparkly

125

leotards with no protest—on the condition that I gave it 100%. And I did. I was all in.

Very little in the gymnastics world came easily for me. I was not bendy. It took me a lot of work and stretching just to do the splits. Lanky and a head taller than the other kids, I had to warm up in order to be ready to warm up, but I kept with it and ended up performing in some local meets where I thankfully was accepted. My parents kept coming and supporting me. The one who finally broke the news to me that five-foot-ten-inch-girls aren't meant for gymnastics was my gymnastics coach. Sweet guy. He convinced me to quit.

But I say I *finished* gymnastics, because quitting implies loss. I have a few trophies and ribbons and as a 46-year-old I can still do a backflip, so there's that. I have come to the following conclusion about finishing: the difference between *finishing* and *quitting* comes down to what's been gained or what is able to be given.

Two roads diverged in a wood. Was one right and the other wrong?

There will come a point when you have to say, I've traveled down this road and it's been great, but this is as far as I go. Time to pick a new path. Is that fickle? Or is that frugal?

Right roads will always have obstacles. Big ones. Wrong roads start out smooth and easy, but eventually, their wrongness will be revealed one way or another. When you select a project that is good and right, you WILL get stuck, thwarted, outright barred. At that point you have two choices: ride it out or re-route. There are two ways to "finish." Most commonly viewed by society is the achievement of a targeted goal. Second, is to acknowledge what's gained, and choose a new course.

How, then, do you reconcile the concepts of perseverance and self-preservation? If the road gets bumpiest just before a break-through, how do you know if you should persevere, or if the bumps are a sign you're on the wrong road? See if these quotes point you toward an acceptable answer.

"Success does not lie in sticking to things.
It lies in picking the right thing to stick to
and quitting the rest."
Annie Duke

"You have to be willing to quit in order to grow."
John Maxwell

Don't mistake no for never. Maybe you need to put a part of your life on hold. Maybe you need to put it on the magic, clarifying shelf. When you come back to it, honor its rightness or wrongness. Act on that clarity immediately before it gets fuzzy again. If and when you realize it's not for you, have the courage to throw it out.

It can be difficult to know when you're meant for a new course or destination. When you get an idea for a new start, check yourself. The real question and challenge is knowing when you are meant to endure and when you're meant to shift. And that is a question only you can answer. But with a better understanding of identity and goals, you have the tools to make that decision.

Finishing may be out of our personal control, so understand that there's a time to be tenacious and a time to be more flexible. Then act accordingly.

QUITTING

In Gallup's 2023 "State of the American Worker" report, a mere 39% of Americans believed they were making meaningful progress toward their long-term goals. Notice this isn't the "achieving" or "finishing" statistic, this only tracks who thinks they're on track. It's a more telling number, because finish lines aren't always in our control. The aim, the position, and the current steps, however, are telling. So, what are the implications of that percentage? Should we feel bad about that number? What would make it higher? Is there a way to close the gap between our present production and our goals?

Culturally, there's such a negative association with quitting, but it needs to be challenged. When it comes to finishing, the paradigm has two outcomes. The most common assessment of a finish is completion of a goal, or the hitting of a target—success! Anything short of that doesn't count. But what if we shift the paradigm. What if you were meant to stop and try something different? Are you the little engine that kept on chugging along? The tortoise who kept a steady course? Or are you made of something different?

> *"When someone is seeking," said Siddartha, "It happens quite easily that he only sees the thing that he is seeking; that he is unable to find anything, unable to absorb anything, because he is only thinking of the thing he is seeking, because he has a goal, because he is obsessed with his goal. Seeking means: to have a goal; but finding means: to be free, to be receptive, to have no goal. You, O worthy one, are perhaps indeed a seeker, for in striving towards your goal, you do not see many things that are under your nose."*[46]

The story of the Buddha as written by Hermann Hesse is a compelling example of defining one's own path and finish line. Siddartha ("Buddha") leaves his comfortable path of worldly success to chart his own course and discover a truer identity and purpose. His destination? Enlightenment. Establishing that state of nirvana, or awakening, as a finish has inspired nearly a billion others to seek the same ultimate goal.

———— • ————

When you feel like quitting but know you shouldn't... give. In 2024 I set a goal to create and then give away twelve new works of art. It was my most productive and well-received year as an artist, and I didn't make a dime.

After the many years of pursuing excellence in painting, there are days I wonder if I should have persisted. My mother, her mother and even back to my great grandmother were all excellent painters, and I was drawn to it. I spent years working under the tutelage of a renowned artist in the Classical Academic genre of realism. He was highly sought, and he chose me as an apprentice. I had an obligation because of the opportunity, didn't I?

Though good reasons to persist, these aren't my reasons because they don't support who I am meant to be—at least, not right now. And who's in control anyway? The only obligation we have is to our own identity and who God made us to be. For the sake of both identity and action, we must be willing to relinquish wrong pursuits in order to regain control.

So caught somewhere between perseverance and quitting, I decided to call my art a hobby—a talent I had acquired. I was obligated to share, not exploit it. I re-drew my finish line.

When you're confronted with a stumbling block, how do you know if you're supposed to find a way around it or if it's a sign you're meant for another path? When you're coached to do something you're uncomfortable with in order to succeed, how do you know if it's time to stretch or stay true to what's in your safe zone? Do you trust an instructor and their process, or do you have confidence in what you've decided? How do you know when the best course is to just say, "not today?"

To check, ask how long it's been since you prayed. Have you been giving? Have you kept your commitments to others and yourself? If the assessment is favorable, trust your gut. If the assessment is poor, discard the idea and amend where you fell short on the assessment.

So *when you've assessed that it's okay to quit* and a U-turn is in order, close the door. No need to call it quitting. Call it finishing.

WHEN IT'S OKAY

This isn't just about personal satisfaction, letting go of misaligned goals frees you to channel your energy into productive pursuits that align with your purpose. This is again why identity is so important as a means. When the direction you're headed is in opposition to who you are and who you're meant to be, it's time to quit.

Maybe you need to quit a hobby that's taking too much of your productive time. Maybe you need to quit a toxic relationship. Maybe you need to quit giving up on yourself... so you can get started.

We are meant to change. So adjustments should be celebrated, even when it means a plan didn't work out. An optimist by nature, I lean toward movement, scoring, offense, and focusing on things you can control rather than worrying about defense and planning for things you can't. But the beauty of a game is that so much happens at once. Any good team knows if you focus on offense or defense singly, you'll lose.

This was illustrated to me perfectly in an intense game of laser tag. Our family got lumped into a group of other people, so we were playing against strangers. I had a fail-proof plan though.

It wasn't my first rodeo and I'd seen before a perfect hideout where someone could just camp out and pick off opponents who passed by from a sniper-like position. It was in a corner of the room (reducing the area to defend), on a platform (higher ground), and had walls on both the open sides with just a narrow passage for entry. I could defend that entry through a small opening or window in one of the walls where I could watch for enemies to approach and eliminate them as they came. Simple philosophy: Just play a good defense.

I lasted about two minutes, only ever getting a shot at two opponents before an enemy approached my fortress. She came in hard and fast, so fast I was only able to get one shot off... and miss. She was now in my fortress, and I was pinned with nowhere to run. She took me out quickly, then, like a sadistic maniac, stayed. She kept her gun on me waiting for my jacket to reboot so she could hit me again the second it popped on. And much as I didn't want to abandon my fortress, the only chance I had at success was to bail.

See the flaw to my plan? Is it possible a good defense is *not* the best offense? I was only concerned about staying safe. I wasn't willing to take any risks, I just wanted to sit back and react to what came my way. I learned the hard way that finishing requires movement, not stasis. Action truly beats reaction, every time.

It's okay to give up on bad plans. It's okay to reposition yourself or start over. Quitting does not erase all you've gained, it allows you to gain differently. Change is the purpose and design of our existence on earth so be gracious and accept what you've gained, then shift your focus.

Quitting isn't failure—it's strategy. By letting go of disconnected goals, you make space for meaningful pursuits that align with your identity.

WHEN IT'S NOT OKAY

While there are times when it's okay to quit, there are certainly times when it's not. Two of the biggest impediments to false-starting are also huge obstacles to bad-finishing. And just as there are wrong reasons to start and not start, there are wrong reasons to finish or not finish.

Fear and pride are nemeses of a good finish. Fear can paralyze you with overthinking or self-doubt, while pride shines a spotlight in all the wrong places. Neither trait is fit for a starter... or a finisher. Let's take a look.

Fear

> *"Fears are educated into us, and can,*
> *if we wish, be educated out."*
> Karl A. Meninger

Fear influences movement in every aspect. It doesn't just mess up our starting, it also messes up finishing.

As a cause, fear will compel you to move. But as mentioned

131

in the chapter on Action, it's not a sustainably productive reason. Quite the contrary. Fear can be very destructive...in finishing as well. Remember the concrete ball? It's scary to jump in front of that thing when it's rolling, and difficult to turn it around, and disappointing to let it roll on without you. But sometimes the courage to do so is exactly what's in order.

There are different types of fear that can cause you to quit prematurely. Fear of success can be a sign you're too worried about how others see you. Careful. That's pride. What about fear of missing out? What you think you're missing is probably inaccurate anyway, especially if your intel stems from social media where perception is delusional. What you anticipate is not reality, so where are your priorities?

Do you tend to overthink about ripple effects? Do you ruminate over implications? Are you concerned about the sacrifices or discomfort you'll endure? Then your cause isn't worth much to you. There are also plenty of fears that keep you from quitting when you should. No matter how your fears are justified, embrace uncertainty and take control back. Don't let fear delay your start or your finish.

QUIT BECAUSE
IT'S WRONG,
NOT BECAUSE
IT'S HARD.

Simplify the rule: Never make a decision based on fear. Keep in mind the certain bumpiness of the road right before you reach the destination. Just before you breakthrough, there will be incredible resistance. Have the guts to follow through, or have the guts to accept when it's truly time to quit.

Pride

This type of fear is quite sneaky but make no mistake, fear of what others think is still fear at its core. It just goes by another name—pride. And it is terribly motivating.

Where does the negative association of quitting stem from? Pride. No one wants to be a "quitter." In my laser tag game, when my defenses had been breached, I sure wanted to persist. I was ready to persist, but I was owned. I could have stayed in my fortress and held my ground. But I would have been eliminated.

Similar to fear, pride focuses outside of our control. It highlights perception. And, like fear, it affects both starting and finishing. When you find yourself hesitant to act, you can usually find the cause to be rooted in pride. When it comes to finishing, whether you finish by reaching your target or by changing course, always beware of pride. It sneaks in when you succeed and when you fail and everything in between.

Every "elimination" suggestion within these pages will chip away at your pride. But now it's time to really squash it. Understand that the type of "pride" being defined here is wholly negative, something to avoid at all costs. This pride is totally self-serving. It shows no regard for the end that justifies its means.

Individuals in any type of leadership position should learn to, like a good coach, reward effort over achievement. To celebrate any progress, no matter how small, rather than criticize where goals weren't met or where the subject fell short. But how well do we apply this practice to ourselves? When we become too fixated on a finish line, we lose track of what we've gained. Our pride keeps us on paths we should've left long ago. It keeps us from quitting when we should.

Don't not quit because of pride. Like rising dough, pride puffs up with nothing but air. It's insubstantial, unsustainable and terribly

133

unsafe. Whether it's your business, a relationship, a goal you've publicized, education or potential advancement, have the humility to be done.

✓ Starters realize both their infinite worth, and profound expendability

A sixth of this book is dedicated to realizing identity. That seems like it points to pride, but the purpose of identity is not to serve self, it's to understand what unique abilities you have to make a difference around you.

There is a wrong kind of confidence, and it stems from pride. It's the confidence that depends on external validation, and is always to our detriment. It is a liability not an asset. Pride is giving yourself too much credit. That's dangerous. When someone tells you, "I'm proud of you", it feels good, right? But who's in control? I'm not saying it's harmful to tell someone you're proud of them, or that you should not feel great when it's directed at you—but lean in a little. What do they have to be proud of? Accept the offering, reciprocate a compliment if they've made an impact on you, but don't give away control.

How do we bridge humility and self-worth? By understanding pride. Pride is all inward, and thus, suffocating. Humility is outward, giving yourself over completely to purpose. Sometimes it's restraint and sometimes it's action, but always it takes effort. Humility is not, as many portray, hiding in the shadows. It's doing your absolute best. It's having the courage to start when you don't feel ready. And knowing when to stop, even if your ball is rolling. Which leads to one more reason it's not okay to quit. Commitments.

Remember in school when you had a horrible teacher in a horrible class that you hated that you would have given anything to drop? Remember that game you were losing so bad you wanted to give up? Remember when you volunteered to help someone but when the time came around it was extremely inconvenient?

134

✓ Starters can be counted on

Especially when someone else is involved, do your best to honor the commitments you've made. You'll be tougher, wiser, and most important will build integrity. The time to reevaluate your involvement is after the commitment ends. Communicate new intentions clearly, find replacements, finish strong. But honor yourself as well. In other words, don't carry on so far that you enable them or disrespect you.

All of us commit to things we shouldn't. No matter the reason you made the deal, keep in mind there may be others equal to your task. Don't make the mistake of thinking you're more important than you are.

Starters know how to finish because they know how and when to quit. They quit when the goal doesn't align with their identity. They aren't afraid to say, "No, that's not who I am." Without judgement, without compromise.

SUMMARY
> *"Every new beginning comes from some*
> *other beginning's end."*
> *Dan Wilson*

Finishing is a tactic starters use to ensure their productivity is effective. Finish means having the courage to follow through when those steps disappear. And the courage to be humble and quit when something isn't right.

Consider carefully. Talk things over. There is only so much time and energy allotted to you. One of the biggest roadblocks to productivity is distraction. Check your schedule and begin to eliminate things that are not necessary or productive. Ask yourself why it's on your calendar. Don't be flaky. Keep your commitments and then as you move forward, learn to unapologetically say no in the first place.

135

Starters know the art of finishing. Win or lose they finish with grace, integrity and humility. *To finish* is a more difficult definition than *to start*. It's in the nature of starters to try a lot of things but no one can do it all. If you hang on a little too tight it can be damaging. It can stop you from finishing something else. In those instances, there can be honor in quitting and knowing when, with discretion and power, to say no. There's no shame in quitting when something is not right for you.

According to U.S. Bureau of Labor Statistics, only 45% of new businesses make it five years. Only 35% make it to ten. It's not easy to start up a business, most don't just happen on a whim. Frankly, can you imagine why anyone would intentionally deal with the paperwork alone unless they were really driven and optimistic about their business succeeding? Reports and analytics on these numbers are generally negative, focusing on why so many fail.

Instead, what if we ask why they started? Redefining the objective may redefine success. Alignment between your goals and identity is as important as the strength of that identity-foundation. The value of a goal is in the reaching, which is why it's so important to focus on progress, not just the end. You can't reach that end without attending to the step in front of you.

Finishing tends to be ambiguous but that's no problem... *for starters.*

So get finished.

Conclusion

This is a visual deception known as the Coffer illusion. Geometrically dominant, it appears at first to consist of all vertical and horizontal lines. The eye assumes it is seeing a bunch of rectangles, but when you shift your focus a little, sixteen perfect circles emerge.

Anthony Norcia[47]

Productivity tends to be viewed as all squares. The checklist of goals, time management, persistence, etc. are widely noted and applied. But nuanced within these critical skills are principles that will make or break how you level up. My dad has said many times,

"Don't let the rulebook get in the way of doing the right thing."

Once you see the circles in the illusion, it's actually difficult to unsee them. Ingrain the six steps you've learned here into your everyday routine until they become second nature. Be grateful, be certain of yourself and your team, master control and keep moving, be a giver not a taker, and attain the art of finishing.

You should have noticed by now that these six principles depend on one another. You could think of them as a cycle. In keynotes I set them up as a day cycle: wake up with gratitude, check the mirror for your identity, acknowledge your team, get moving, make sure your movements are outward, conquer the day. Repeat. But more than cyclical, or linear, embrace them as connected, intertwined, and totally interdependent.

How's your fire doing? Is it prepped? Are you still holding the match? What are you waiting for?

"Happiness is where you start, not where you finish."
Four-time Olympian, gold medalist, Dan Jansen

As a starter, you are counted on to do your best and make a positive ripple. Starters have the biggest impact.

That **Impact** comes from:
- Being certain of your **I**dentity
- Controlling your **M**ovement
- Maximizing **P**roductivity
- Having an **A**ttitude of gratitude
- Intentionally **C**ontributing
- Knowing your **T**eam

Those who start will forever lead those who wait. So become what you were born to become, a starter. The world needs you.

- ✓ Starters use what's available to them to make a lasting change

- ✓ Starters are grateful

- ✓ Starters are creators

- ✓ Starters know their team

- ✓ Starters put the team goal first

- ✓ Starters don't stop moving

- ✓ Starters own their mistakes

- ✓ Starters don't react, they act

- ✓ Starters are comfortable with being uncomfortable

- ✓ Starters are the best benchwarmers

- ✓ Starters make no excuses

- ✓ Starters realize both their infinite worth, and profound expendability

- ✓ Starters can be counted on

References

1. Gail Matthews. 2007. *Goals research summary.* Dominican University of California. https://www.dominican.edu/sites/default/files/2020-02/gailmatthews-harvard-goals-researchsummary.pdf

2. Brown, J. Wong, J. 2017. *How gratitude changes you and your brain.* Greater Good Magazine. https://greatergood.berkeley.edu/article/item/how_gratitude_changes_you_and_your_brain

3. Harvard Health Publishing. 2021. *Giving thanks can make you happier...* Harvard Medical School. https://www.health.harvard.edu/healthbeat/giving-thanks-can-make-you-happier

4. Psychology Today. 2014. *7 scientifically proven benefits of gratitude.* Journal of Applied Sport Psychology. https://www.psychologytoday.com/us/blog/what-mentally-strong-people-dont-do/201504/7-scientifically-proven-benefits-of-gratitude

5. Iodice, et al. 2021. *The association between gratitude and depression.* University of New England, Australia. Clinmed Journals. https://clinmedjournals.org/articles/ijda/international-journal-of-depression-and-anxiety-ijda-4-024.php?jid=ijda#res

6. Fredrickson, B.L., et al. 2003. *What good are positive emotions in a crisis.* Journal of Personality and Social Psychology, *84*(2), 365–376.

7. Psychology Today. 2015. *7 Scientifically proven benefits of gratitude.* https://www.psychologytoday.com/us/blog/what-mentally-strong-people-dont-do/201504/7-scientifically-proven-benefits-of-gratitude.

8. Dewall, N. et al. 2012. *A grateful heart is a nonviolent heart: Cross-sectional, experience sampling, longitudinal, and experimental evidence.* Social Psychological and Personality Science 3(2):232-240.

9. Greater Good Magazine. 2017. How Gratitude Changes You And Your Brain. Greater Good Science Center. https://greatergood.berkeley.edu/article/item/how_gratitude_changes_you_and_your_brain

10. Amie Gordon. 2012. To have and to hold: Gratitude promotes relationship maintenance in intimate bonds. National Library of Medicine. https://pubmed.ncbi.nlm.nih.gov/22642482/

11. Journal of Psychosomatic Research. 2020. A systematic review of gratitude interventions: Effects on physical health and health behaviors. Elsevier. https://www.sciencedirect.com/science/article/abs/pii/S0022399920301847

12. Logan, A. 2022. Mayo Clinic. *Can expressing gratitude improve your mental, physical health?* https://www.mayoclinichealthsystem.org/hometown-health/speaking-of-health/can-expressing-gratitude-improve-health

13. Science Direct. 2023. *Personality and individual differences.* Elsevier. https://www.sciencedirect.com/science/article/abs/pii/S0191886922004287

14. Andrews. 2011. *How gratitude helps you sleep at night.* Psychology Today. https://www.psychologytoday.com/us/blog/minding-the-body/201111/how-gratitude-helps-you-sleep-at-night

15. Emmons. McCullough. 2003. *Counting Blessings Versus Burdens: An Experimental Investigation of Gratitude and Subjective Well-Being in Daily Life.* Journal of Personality and Social Psychology 84(2):377-389

16. Zakrzewski, V. 2016. *How humility will make you the greatest person ever.* Greater Good Science Center. https://greatergood.berkeley.edu/article/item/humility_will_make_you_greatest_person_ever

17.Wirtz, D., Gordon, C. L., & Stalls, J. 2014. Religion and spirituality across cultures. 287–301. Springer Science + Business Media.

18.Wood, Froh, and Geraghty. 2010. *Gratitude and Well-being. A review and theoretical integration.* Elsevier https://www.sciencedirect.com/science/article/abs/pii/S0272735810000450

19.Zimmer. 2014-present. *The one you feed with Emiliya Zhivotovskaya. https://www.oneyoufeed.net/emiliya-zhivotovskaya/*

20.Seligman, Steen, Park, Peterson. 2005. *Positive psychology progress: empirical validation of interventions. Am Psychol.* https://pubmed.ncbi.nlm.nih.gov/16045394/

21.Sexton, Adair. *Forty-five good things: a prospective pilot study of the Three Good Things well-being intervention in the USA for healthcare worker emotional exhaustion, depression, work–life balance and happiness.* BMJ Journal. https://bmjopen.bmj.com/content/9/3/e022695

22. Office of Community Planning and Development. 2022. *The 2022 Annual Homeless Assessment Report (AHAR) to Congress.* pg.4. The U.S. Department of Housing and Urban Development

23. USDA Economic Research Service. 2024. *Food Secuity in the U.S. - Key Statistics & Graphics.* United Statees Department of Agriculture. https://www.ers.usda.gov/topics/food-nutrition-assistance/food-security-in-the-us/key-statistics-graphics#:~:text=12.2%20million%20adults%20lived%20in%20households%20with,more%20child%20experienced%20very%20low%20food%20security.

24. Homelessness Statistics. 2024. State of Homelessness 2024 Edition. *https://endhomelessness. org/homelessness-in-america/homelessness-statistics/state-of-homelessness/.* National Alliance to End Homelessness

25. Feeding America. 2023. 1 in 6 people received help from charitable food sector in 2022. https://www.feedingamerica.org/about-us/press-room/Charitable-Food-Assistance-2022

26.National Institutes of Health (US); Biological Sciences Curriculum Study. 2007. *Understanding Human Genetic Variation.* National Library of Medicine. https://www.ncbi.nlm.nih.gov/books/NBK20363/

27.UN Chronicle. 2024. *Multilingual Education: A key to quality and inclusive learning.* United Nations. https://www.un.org/en/un-chronicle/multilingual-education-key-quality-and-inclusive-learning

28. Health Psychol. 2013. Personality and the Leading Behavioral Contributors of Mortality

29.Mashasi Soga et al. 2016. *Gardening is beneficial for health: A meta-analysis.* National Library of Medicine. https://pmc.ncbi.nlm.nih.gov/articles/PMC5153451/

30. Gepp. 2022. *Benefits of a flow state.* Medical News Today. https://www.medicalnewstoday.com/articles/flow-state

31.Shakespeare. 1603. *Hamlet IV:V.* Houghton Mifflin

32.English Translation of the Meaning of Al-Qur'An. 1997. *Surah Hud 42-43*

33.Doris Kearns Goodwin. 2005. *Team of rivals: Lincoln's political genius.* Simon & Schuster

34.United States Census Bureau. 2024. *Census Bureau Releases New Estimates on Families and Living Arrangements.* https://www.census.gov/newsroom/press-releases/2024/families-living-arrangements.html#:~:text=Additionally%2C%20nonfamily%20households%20were%20about%2019%25%20of,alone%2C%20compared%20to%20about%2016%25%20in%202022.

35.Theodore Roosevelt. 1910. *Speech at Sorbonne, Paris*

36.Merriam Webster. (n.d.) *Fear. Merriam-Webster.com dictionary.* Retrieved on March 2, 2023, from https://www.merriam-webster.com/dictionary/fear

37.fGavin DeBecker. 2010. *The gift of fear: survival signals that protect us from violence.* DeBecker

38.John Blofeld. 2000. *Taoism; the road to immortality.* Shambhala Boston

39. Moore (Director). 2012. *Wreck it Ralph.* Walt Disney Animation Studios

40.Anna Lembke. 2021. *Dopamine Nation: Finding balance in the age of indulgence.* Dutton Books

41. King James Version Bible. 1993. Jeremiah 1:8

42. McChesney, Huling, Covey. 2012. *Four disciplines of execution: achieving your wildly important goals.* Free Press

43. King James Version Bible. 1993. Isaiah 61:3

44.ResearchGate. Dunn. 2008. *Spending money on others creates happiness. https://www.researchgate.net/ publication/5494996_Spending_Money_on_Others_Promotes_Happiness*

45. World Health Organization. 2023. *Drinking water.* https://www.who.int/news-room/fact-sheets/detail/drinking-water

46.Hesse. 2008. *Siddhartha.* Simon & Schuster

47.Anthony Norcia (Artist). 2006

Heather Jo Kennedy is a Certified Professional Coach, two-time author, and inspirational speaker. After graduating Cum Laude from Utah State University, she has built multiple businesses which continue to operate along the Utah Wasatch Front. Heather is passionate about teamwork and productivity. She uses her formula in "For Starters" to help leaders and teams of all industries achieve their highest levels of cohesion and performance. Call her coach, foodie, adventurer, lover of animals and all things chocolate. But above all, she is a mama bear.

Find Heather at www.hjkennedy.com

www.ingramcontent.com/pod-product-compliance
Lightning Source LLC
Chambersburg PA
CBHW071751120626
46550CB00002B/749